LISA BRENNINKMEYER

Walking with Purpose

SEVEN PRIORITIES THAT MAKE LIFE WORK

D0038709

 **DynamicCatholic.com**
Be Bold. Be Catholic.®

WALKING WITH PURPOSE

FIRST EDITION

Copyright © 2013 Lisa Brenninkmeyer

Published by Beacon Publishing.

Soft Cover ISBN 978-1-937509-44-6

Hard Cover ISBN 978-1-937509-43-9

Dynamic Catholic® and Be Bold. Be Catholic.®
are registered trademarks of The Dynamic Catholic Institute.

Book Cover Design by:
Jillian Buhl • Melissa Overmyer • Allison Taylor

For more information on this title and other books and CDs
available through the Dynamic Catholic Book Program,
please visit: www.DynamicCatholic.com

The Dynamic Catholic Institute
2200 Arbor Tech Drive
Hebron, KY 41048
Phone 1–859–980–7900
Email: info@DynamicCatholic.com

Printed in the United States of America.

Table of Contents

This book is dedicated to *Julie Ricciardi,*
my dear friend and tireless partner in ministry.
I'm better for knowing you (Proverbs 27:17).
I'm so grateful that you love
Walking with Purpose as much as I do.

"Two are better than one,
because they have a good reward for their toil.
For if they fall, one will lift up his fellow;
but woe to him who is alone when he falls
and has not another to lift him up."
Ecclesiastes 4:9-10

Introduction

If you picked up this book hoping to learn how to walk with purpose from someone who has completely figured out life, I might disappoint you a little. If you want to listen to someone whose decisions are always wise and well thought out, then my decision to add a fifty-pound puppy to our already busy family mix might rule me out as a candidate. Let me digress for a moment and just say that a fifty-pound puppy is a very large animal. When you already have seven children and all the paraphernalia that accompanies them, a wise choice would be a smaller creature. Before you judge me, may I say that I actually meant to buy a much smaller dog. And I thought I had. But when I went for my first vet visit, I was told that we had a *very large* puppy. "Oh, no," I assured her. "She's not going to be large. She's only going to come up to my knee. That's why I picked this breed." The vet looked at me quizzically, and asked if I had seen the parents and grandparents of our puppy. I had not, but I pointed out that her ancestors were standard poodles, therefore *small*. She quickly corrected me by showing me a photo of a standard poodle, which is actually quite large. But by this point, Bailey the puppy was a member of the family, and I could hardly cause my children untold trauma by returning her to the breeder.

One would think that this would have taught me the very important lesson of tending to details—*every* detail, or you never know what might happen. But then a storm hit our city, and we lost electricity for more than a week. This meant that we didn't have water—we couldn't flush toilets, take a shower, or otherwise enjoy life. In the midst of this, Bailey got an ear infection, and her ears needed to be diligently treated with ointment twice a day and then dutifully massaged. And in my defense, this is what I did. And I was very proud of myself, since I find it hard to remember to keep giving my children their antibiotics all the way to the very end of the dose. But the devil is in the details, and after five days of commenting that she seemed to be getting worse, not better, and seeing her continually shaking her head like a maniac, I realized that I had been using superglue instead of antibiotic ointment. Bailey survived the ordeal, but whenever she won't come when we call her, the kids just look at me with raised eyebrows.

I struggle with getting my act together, just like you do. We all experience some days that are like the sweet spot on the tennis racket. We wake up in a good mood after a full night's sleep, everyone in the family eats well, we cross off everything on our to-do lists, and no major crisis occurs. But more often than not, life doesn't go that smoothly.

There are a lot of days when we don't get enough sleep. We eat what's left on our children's plates. We overschedule ourselves, then rush around and arrive late. Kids have dirty diapers just when we need to walk out the door. Money is tight. Loved ones get cancer. Spouses are unfaithful. All these circumstances can tempt us to say, "I'll start exploring how God wants me to be living the day things slow down and are a little more under control."

I want to encourage you not to wait for that day. Instead, I'd like you to see today as the perfect time to begin walking with purpose. Why? Because what you are experiencing is real life. We may occasionally have times when things are perfectly under control, but we need to learn how to walk with purpose regardless of our circumstances. Each season of life carries with it chaos and troubles. If a calm schedule is the prerequisite for purposeful, peaceful living, we will never achieve it. Whether you find yourself in a period of calm or chaos, why not join me as, together, we begin to walk with purpose?

Section One

PUTTING SOME BASICS IN PLACE

Walking with purpose requires that we come to grips with what ultimately matters. We need to understand why we are here on earth. The reason we are here is far bigger than personal fulfillment, inner peace, or happiness. It's bigger than raising a family or having a career. The reason we are here is because God wanted us to be here. You were made *by* God and *for* God. If we don't look at life from that perspective, nothing will make sense.

This is what Saint Paul had to say about his life focus:

> It is not that I have already taken hold of it or have already attained perfect maturity, but I continue my pursuit in hope that I may possess it, since I have indeed been taken possession of by Christ [Jesus]. Brothers, I for my part do not consider myself to have taken possession. Just one thing: Forgetting what lies behind but straining forward to what lies ahead, I continue my pursuit toward the goal, the prize of God's upward calling in Christ Jesus.[1]

Saint Paul wasn't saying that he had it all perfectly together. But he kept his eye on the goal. He knew that God was calling him to something better. He wasn't going to turn back. Instead, he was determined to focus on the prize so that he could experience everything that God had planned for him.

Saint Paul's faithfulness to God, focus on his mission, and determination not to compromise literally changed the world. He didn't do this by floating along the river of life, letting his circumstances guide him. If we want to be women who walk purposefully and experience all that God has for us in this life, then we, like Saint Paul, are going to need to focus and prioritize. There simply isn't enough time in the day to do everything that your loved ones tell you is important and the things that our culture values, and still do the things that God is calling you to do. If you're interested in joining me on the journey, you will have to make choices—like what to pack for the trip.

One of my favorite getaways is Camden, Maine. I could write a very interesting journal full of packing mishaps for those trips—like my twelve-year-old announcing, five days into the trip, that he had forgotten to pack any underwear. It's funny (at least looking back on it) when it's my kids who didn't pack well. It's just plain embarrassing when I'm traveling alone and I have no one to blame but myself for what's not in my suitcase. We all realize how important it is to have the basics with us when we leave on a trip. Walking with purpose, in that sense, is no different from any other journey. Before we set out, then, let me suggest four essentials that we want to have packed away for the journey:

1. Understanding the Depth of God's Love

2. Recognizing What Drives You

3. Avoiding Distractions

4. Cultivating an Eternal Perspective

ESSENTIAL #1:
UNDERSTANDING THE DEPTH OF GOD'S LOVE

I believe that we will never be focused and centered on Christ until we are convinced that he loves us. It is statistically proven that we respond better when motivated by love and a close relationship than when driven by fear of consequences.

Many things get in the way of our really believing that God loves us. We tend to attribute to God the characteristics of our earthly fathers. If your father wasn't loving, you may find it hard to believe that your Heavenly Father loves you unconditionally.

Or perhaps you have been deeply hurt by circumstances in your life. Your suffering makes it hard for you to believe that God really loves you—if he did, then why would he have allowed certain hardships to happen? We can't see God, and most of us do not hear his audible voice, so our doubts continue.

Sometimes it is guilt that gets in the way of believing God loves us. We look at our past and think that God couldn't possibly love us when we have so repeatedly failed to live the way he desires.

When we find ourselves dwelling on these doubts, we need to realign our thinking with what is true. The truth is that not only did God make you—you are his masterpiece! He looks at you and is thrilled with what he has made.

Michelangelo's magnificent *Pietà* now stands in St. Peter's Basilica, in Rome. The sculpture portrays the serenity and strength of the Virgin Mary as she holds the crucified Christ in her arms. The story is told that Michelangelo was criticized for sculpting the Virgin Mary with such a young face. At the time of Christ's death, she would have been much older, so this artistic choice seemed foolish and inaccurate. Michelangelo replied by telling his critics that when he depicted the Virgin's face, he had carved the image of his precious mother, who had died when he was only five. The *Pietà* poured out of Michelangelo's heart, and there was nothing he would do to change it. It was the only sculpture that Michelangelo signed, as if to say, "This is mine. This reflects my heart. I can't prevent you from criticizing it, but this is my masterpiece."

I wonder if that is what God wants to tell us when we don't look at ourselves the way he sees us? He sees that there are things we'd like to change about ourselves, but that doesn't make us any less the apple of his eye. No matter what your parents or other children may have said to you as you grew up, or your husband, or anyone else, God is completely captivated by you. He loves you. Speaking through Isaiah the prophet, God says, "You are precious in my eyes and honored, and I love you."[2] Later, in the book of Zechariah, we are told, "He who touches you touches the apple of [God's] eye."[3] He is on your side. There is nothing that he would not do for you, which is for your good.

We have a hard time understanding that kind of love. But occasionally, we are able to get a glimpse of it in other people. There was a family dentist in Seattle, Dr. Reddick. He was known as an unusually kind and sensitive man. He was an experienced mountain climber and was camping on Mount Rainier with two of his four children in midsummer. Moving from one camp to another, they were caught by a sudden summer blizzard. Dr. Reddick burrowed a cave in the snow, put his children in the back, and lay across the opening to keep the fierce cold away from them. His children recounted later how he comforted them and told them familiar Bible stories. But as the storm raged on, he slowly froze to death, all the while comforting and protecting his children.[4] This is the kind of love that Christ has for you. Even his own life was not more precious to him than yours. Do you feel unworthy of that kind of love?

A Brazilian pastor told the story of a young widow whose beautiful teenage daughter felt that life in their rural village was limiting. She longed for the excitement of Rio de Janeiro. Her mother knew how often dreams turned to disappointment, as jobs in the city were scarce. It was typically a short journey to desperation and the willingness to make money in whatever way a young, pretty girl could. She continually tried to discourage her daughter from going to the big city. But one morning, she was devastated to find that her precious daughter was gone. All that remained was a note.

So the mother packed her bag, took all the money she could, and went to the bus station to go after her daughter. While she waited for the bus to come, she took picture after picture of herself in a little photo booth. She wrote a note on the back of each photo and filled her purse with them. Once she arrived in Rio, she went from place to place, looking everywhere she could think of for her daughter. She started with the places she hoped she'd find her, but then turned to the places where she feared she might be. Each time she visited a bar, nightclub, or hotel, she left one of the photo booth pictures of herself tacked to the wall or a bathroom mirror. But it wasn't long before her money and photos ran out, and she had to go home, carrying the heaviness of failure in her heart.

A few weeks later, in one of the hotels often visited by streetwalkers and prostitutes, her daughter slowly walked down the stairs. Her eyes no longer sparkled. She no longer had dreams of the life a big city could offer her. She was living a nightmare. But she knew that no matter how much she wanted to, she could never go home. Not now. Her eye caught something familiar. It was a photograph of her mother. Incredulous, she walked over to the wall and pulled the photo down. On the back, she read the note from her mother: "Whatever you are, whatever you've become, it doesn't matter. Please, come home." She did.

Perhaps you need to hear those words from Christ today. "Whatever you have done, whatever you've become, it doesn't matter. Please come home and discover God's love for you." There is no sin greater than God's mercy. There is nothing unforgivable. God waits, longing to cleanse and restore you. He loves you with an everlasting, unfading, unconditional love.

ESSENTIAL #2:
RECOGNIZING WHAT DRIVES YOU

Even when we desire with all our hearts to do what we know is right, we find ourselves making the wrong choices time and time again. We aren't alone in this. Saint Paul wrote in Romans 7:15, "I do not understand my own actions. For I do not do what I want, but I do the very thing I hate." Can you relate? How many of us wake up in the morning determined to be pleasant to our husbands and children all day long, only to find we aren't able to make it to lunch without showing our irritation?

If we want to reorient our lives more toward God, then we need to get under the layer of our behavior to the motivation that leads to that behavior. We need to determine what drives us. Ideally, we will be driven or motivated by a pure love for God. Our desire will be to please him in all things, and for him to get the credit for any good we do. That is our ideal.

But more often than not, we are motivated by a love not for God, but for ourselves. It is our instinct to look out for ourselves, but the way we do this varies from person to person.

The Catholic Church wants to help us know ourselves better, and the Holy Spirit has given us two thousand years of great understanding and knowledge of the human heart and mind. The better we know ourselves, the more effectively we will become the women that we so desperately want to be.

One of the obstacles in the spiritual life is our ability to justify our wrong behavior—not facing the truth about ourselves and calling a spade a spade. Instead of just looking out for ourselves, we need to look within. There are three common ways we tend to look out for ourselves, typical motives within our hearts that lead to thoughts and then to behavior.

Saint Ignatius of Loyola explored two of them in his Spiritual Exercises. he found that we are primarily motivated by either pride or sensuality. All other sins spring from these two root sins. Father Aloysius Bellecius described them as follows:

"This twofold root consists of principally 1, in a desire of our own excellence—that is to say, in pride; and 2, in a thirst for pleasures, that is sensuality. From these ordinarily spring all sins, both mortal and venial—even those of which the parent is avarice; for we only desire riches insofar as they serve to second our ambitious projects, or to gratify our desires of pleasure."[6]

MOTIVATED BY PRIDE

Some of us are driven by our accomplishments. We live to complete our to-do lists. We become obsessed with our goals. Others' expectations of us are exceeded only by our own expectations of ourselves. On the surface, accomplishing goals strikes us as a virtue. But the true goodness of what we do is found in our motives, and at the root of these achievements, we can find pride. What is the motive behind what we do? Are we doing these things to please God, or to please ourselves? Are we doing them because they are things that God has called us to do, or are we doing them in order to feel more secure with others and pleased with ourselves?

When we are motivated by pride, we recognize in ourselves a need for accomplishment at all costs—often not to please God, but to satisfy our own ego. We struggle with control. Trusting God and relinquishing control to him is especially difficult. Who knows what he might do or allow? Our security is found in our ability to "do it all," and as long as we're hitting the mark, we feel safe and significant.

It's hard to look below the surface at sin, and when we struggle with pride we often rationalize our behavior. We're more likely to see the sin in others than to recognize it in ourselves. But when our sin is staring us in the face, rather than responding with humility, we often dissolve into self-pity.

When we are driven by pride, defining our worth through what we accomplish, finding our security in ourselves, we might find ourselves thinking things like this:

"I have to be perfect."

"Failure is not an option, because if I fail, I am a failure."

"Have I achieved x, y, or z? If not, nothing else matters."

The opposite of pride is faith. Pride sees everything through our own point of view. Faith sees it all through God's perspective. Pride places us at the center. Faith makes God the center of our lives, and makes pleasing him and doing what he desires our greatest goal.

MOTIVATED BY SENSUALITY

Some of us are driven by our desire for comfort and pleasure. We feel good about ourselves when our circumstances are good. We make decisions based on what we feel like doing. Our security is found in our possessions, our level of comfort, and feeling good.

We live in a society driven by materialism, which at its root is a philosophy motivated by sensuality. Blessed John Paul II talked a lot about how we are a society based on having more than being. So what do we do when we are down? We buy something!

When we are motivated by sensuality, we tend to focus on our feelings, emotions, and sentiments. We can become enslaved by our feelings, only doing what we should when we feel like it. Another pitfall of sensuality is a disordered focus on pleasure. Pleasurable things are a problem when we become enslaved to them. We can live to eat. We can live to drink. We can live to go on vacation. We can live to shop.

Sensuality is living for today, for the moment. But as Catholics, we are often challenged to live for tomorrow. We need the virtue of hope to counter the root sin of sensuality.

As you read this, you probably recognize, just like I did, the reality of those two common motives. You may also have noted the reality of a third motive that drives us, particularly in our current culture: our propensity to be motivated by the opinions of others.

MOTIVATED BY THE OPINIONS OF OTHERS

In the lives of many women, the opinion of others has become a common motivator. Instead of seeking security and value in God, we look for other people to measure our worth. When we are motivated by what other people think of us, our actions are driven by our desire for affirmation, to be noticed, and to be praised: "I'll do, so I can be loved." There is a difference between liking to be appreciated and doing something in order to be appreciated. In the latter case, our value is determined by the opinions of others. We become people pleasers—motivated more by what those around us want than by what God is calling us to do and be.

The greatest need of a woman who is driven by others' opinions of her is to be loved. Out of a fear of rejection, we define ourselves by how other people perceive us. God calls us to define ourselves by his unconditional love for us. When we settle for the fickle love of other people, it's harder for us to soak up God's love. Ideally, we will be so filled up by God's love that it can spill over into the lives of those around us, helping us to love as Christ loves. But when we're obsessed with what others think of us, we often struggle to have intimate relationships. Our greatest concern is to be affirmed and validated, and so the temptation is enormous to wear a mask and be whoever we think those around us want us to be.

Oftentimes, when we recognize that we are motivated by others' opinions of us, we find that some of this has come from our relationships with our earthly fathers. If our earthly fathers don't love us unconditionally and communicate that effectively, we will often, as young girls, seek that affirmation from friends. As we get older, we'll seek it in a boyfriend and later, a husband. In these relationships, we are seeking security. We are seeking affirmation that we are worthy of love. When this is what drives us, we desperately need God's unconditional love to fill us.

So I ask myself, which of these three motivations best describes me? It is likely that all three describe me at certain times, but one should describe me more consistently.

There is little benefit to just recognizing where we most commonly fall. The point of getting to know ourselves better is to recognize where we seek security instead of in God. We need to recognize that by seeking worth and security in accomplishments, in things or comfort, or in others' opinions of us, we will always fall short. None of these things can be counted on. All of these can be taken away from us in an instant.

In order to be truly secure, to find our worth in something that can never be taken away, we need to recognize the true source of security and worth. That source lies in a relationship with God. In order to break habits of seeking security in the wrong places, we need to develop the virtues and strengths that are the opposites of our vices and weaknesses.

Let's look at these vices one by one. When we are seeking security and our worth in ourselves, motivated by pride, then we are deficient in **FAITH**. Faith is believing in what we don't see—trusting God even when we don't have answers and things feel out of control. As we grow in faith, we are living out the lesson that our worth comes from God and what he does, not what we accomplish. We recognize that we aren't in control, and that doesn't mean we have to be insecure, because God is in control. These lessons become our own as we grow in faith. Faith is the opposite of **PRIDE**.

When we seek security and worth in things and in our level of comfort, which we call sensuality, we are deficient in **HOPE**. When we are defining our worth and security by the things around us, we are focusing on the here and now. Our eyes are not on eternity. It's all about the present moment. If we want to break away from being driven by sensuality, we need to grow in hope. Hope is what allows us to look to the future, and to experience discomfort in the present in order to gain something better down the road. Hope helps us to break bad habits (even though in the present moment they feel so good), because we're looking to the future and can see how much better it would be if we lived our lives according to what God values. Sometimes God values pain today, if it helps us to have a better tomorrow. A good verse to meditate on in order to grow in hope is 2 Corinthians 4:17: "For this momentary light affliction is producing for us an eternal weight of glory beyond all comparison, as we look not to what is seen but to what is unseen; for what is seen is transitory, but what is unseen is eternal." If we want to stop being driven by sensuality, we need to grow in hope.

When we seek security and worth in other people's opinions of us, we are deficient in love. We're not experiencing the depth of unconditional love that God wants us to experience. We are hoping that the approval and affirmation of people around us will fill us up, but it never will. Only as we understand the depths of God's unconditional love will we be able to let go of the need to please people at all costs—only then can we be free of the tyranny of the opinions of others.

Do you struggle with pride? Allow him to build your faith. Do you struggle with sensuality? Allow him to develop hope in you. Do you struggle with people pleasing? Allow him to convince you of his unconditional love.

ESSENTIAL #3: **AVOIDING DISTRACTIONS**

In her book *A Practical Guide to Prayer,* Dorothy Haskin tells about a noted concert violinist who was asked the secret of her mastery of the instrument. The woman answered the question with two words: "Planned neglect." Then she explained. "There were many things that used to demand my time. When I went to my room after breakfast, I made my bed, straightened the room, dusted, and did whatever seemed necessary. When I finished my work, I turned to my violin practice. That system prevented me from accomplishing what I should on the violin. So I reversed things. I deliberately planned to neglect everything else until my practice period was complete. And that program of planned neglect is the secret of my success."[7]

Most of us have more things expected of us, more things on our plate, than we can possibly get done in a day. We can always do more as friends, as mothers, as wives, in our careers, in our volunteer work. In order for us to be certain that we have time for the things that matter most, we must avoid distractions. Just like the concert violinist, we need to deliberately plan to neglect those nonessentials that get in the way of doing what is most important. If we do not determine which of our activities are the most important and *do those first*, then we will make choices based on circumstances, pressure, and our current mood. The truth is, it's impossible for us to do everything that the people around us want us to do. The demands will prove to be greater than the hours in the day. But God promises us that there is always enough time to do what he is calling us to do.

Whenever I get harried and am tempted to say that I do not have enough time, I tell myself, "There is enough time in the day to accomplish everything God wants me to do. If I am harried, it is because I am doing things that God has not asked of me." When I take the time to analyze why I am doing a certain activity, I often find that I am motivated by pride (doing things because they are personal goals and I want to accomplish them for my glory), or sensuality (doing what I feel like because it's more comfortable or easier), or the opinions of others (doing things that God doesn't expect of me so that people will think more highly of me).

As you look at your daily schedule, ask yourself why you are doing what you do. The key to determining where you should spend your time lies in your motivation and your priorities. Do these things have eternal value? If you were to cut out certain activities, would you be able to find more time to do the things that really matter?

Think of Jesus's example. Who, more than he, had the right to say, "I don't have enough time for everything I need to get done! Everywhere I look there is something else that needs my attention, and I seem to be the only one who can do it! I don't even have time to sleep!" But is that how he responded to the extreme pressures he felt? How did he deal with the fact that he was constantly surrounded by human need and seemingly left many tasks unfinished?

On the night before Jesus died, he said to his Heavenly Father, "I have accomplished the work which you gave me to do." He didn't heal every sick person on earth. When he ascended to heaven, there was still sickness and heartache and pain. But Jesus knew that he had accomplished what his father had called him to do, and that was enough.

How did he know which people to heal, which miracles to perform, which hearts to bind up? The secret lies in Jesus's prayer life and in the focus that resulted. We read in Mark 1:35, "Rising very early before dawn, he left and went off to a deserted place, where he prayed." Each day, Jesus got his marching orders from the Father. When I read that, I wonder at the times I have said that I am too busy to pray. If Jesus needed prayer, why do I act as if I don't?

ESSENTIAL #4: CULTIVATING AN ETERNAL PERSPECTIVE

Jesus was able to avoid nonessential distractions not only because of his laser focus on the essentials of "being about his father's business" but also because of his equally focused sense of what lay ahead. At the height of his popularity, throngs of people followed him, marveling at both his miracles and his words. Even then, he never lost sight of the essential things that lay ahead.

Saint Luke captured this focus when he recorded, "He resolutely determined to go to Jerusalem,"[8] not as another venue for attention and acclaim, but as the place where he would fulfill the ultimate mission that caused his father to send his son—to die on a rough hewn cross to pay the penalty for your sin and mine. And his view of the future extended far beyond next week or next month. He lived with his eyes set on eternity.

Believe me, I know what a challenge it is to cultivate an eternal perspective. On any given morning, I'm thrilled as I'm getting the kids out the door to school if I can think ahead to the balancing act we'll have to manage after school, with activities running us in multiple directions. I know it's not any easier for you. The tyranny of the demands of the moment so often squeezes out any time to even consider eternity, let alone to cultivate an eternal perspective. Yet with all the incredible demands on Jesus's time, demands that never abated, he lived each moment with his eyes and his heart on eternity.

He lifted his focus to the future, to where he was heading. Hebrews 12:2 urges us to keep our "eyes fixed on Jesus, the leader and perfecter of faith. For the sake of the joy that lay before him he endured the cross, despising its shame, and has taken his seat at the right hand of God. Consider how he endured such opposition from sinners, in order that you may not grow weary and lose heart."

Are you weary? Are you losing heart? Many of us may do our best to look pulled together on the outside, but on the inside we feel a quiet desperation. "Is this all there is?" we ask.

"To Americans usually tragedy is wanting something very badly and not getting it," observed Henry Kissinger. "Many people have had to learn in their private lives, and nations have had to learn in their historical experience, that perhaps the worst form of tragedy is wanting something badly, getting it, and finding it empty."[9]

Sometimes our quiet desperation comes from having achieved everything the world says matters, and finding it hasn't delivered on its promises. Sometimes the weariness and desperation come from unmet longings and aching disappointments. In both cases, we must believe that this life is not all there is. There is so much more. It's as if we are standing watching a parade. We want to see what is just around the corner—then we can determine if it's worth sticking around for. But God stands above all. He can see the beginning and what is just around the corner. He knows that there are better things ahead—both here on earth and in heaven.

Some time ago, I spoke to a group of women about priorities. It was my desire to encourage the women to spend their time on the things that mattered, so I gave ideas and encouraged women in those areas. Little did I know that in the midst of that group there was a precious friend of mine who was deeply struggling, wanting to do all of these things that I was talking about but feeling she was unable to do so. Only a month after we were together, she took her own life, shattering her family and our community with grief and shock. How I wish I could turn back the clock and say, "There are better things ahead. Do not lose hope. You have a Heavenly Father who loves you—no matter what you do or do not do. His love for you cannot be diminished. It is unconditional. There is more to this life. Hold on."

God can shine light into the darkness. He can set every prisoner free. He can make streams flow in the desert. Never forget that the darkest hour in the night is the hour before dawn. Just hold on, one more moment. God is in control, even if it feels like he isn't. He is in control, and he loves you. There are better things ahead.

In 1871, Horatio Spafford and his family were living happily in Chicago. During that year, the Great Chicago Fire devastated the area. Two years later, Horatio Spafford decided to take his wife and four daughters on a once in a lifetime trip to France. Horatio was detained on business, but sent his wife and children ahead. Travel across the Atlantic was far more dangerous in those days, and in the middle of the ocean, the ship carrying Horatio's precious wife and children collided with another liner and sank. Two hundred and twenty-six people were lost. Although Horatio's wife survived, all four of their children perished.

Horatio boarded a vessel to travel to Europe to comfort and grieve with his wife. As they sailed across, the captain showed Horatio the very place where the tragedy had occurred. Overwhelmed with grief and pain, Horatio went to his room. Although his loss brought indescribable pain, he also experienced a peace that this world can neither give nor understand. He picked up his pen and composed the words to the familiar hymn "It Is Well with My Soul." He wrote:

> When peace like a river attendeth my way
> When sorrow like sea billows roll

Whatever my lot, Thou hast taught me to say

It is well, it is well with my soul.[10]

Somehow, in the midst of senseless tragedy and pain that we cannot even imagine, this man was able to cling to God, and hope.

The Milan Cathedral reminds everyone who steps inside of this important perspective. As you pass through the first arch over the entrance, you see beautiful carved roses. Underneath, you find the words "All that which pleases is but for a moment."

Passing under the next arch, you observe a sculpted cross and the words "All that which troubles us is but for a moment."

Just before entering the cathedral to worship and commune with Christ, you receive the most important message: "That only is important which is eternal."[11]

God calls us in and asks us to focus on the cross. He asks us to develop an eternal perspective on life. He asks us to turn our eyes to Jesus—our only hope. He is the source of our purpose. He made us. It is only as we make him our all that we can become all he created us to be.

PUTTING YOUR PRIORITIES
IN ORDER

The craziness of Sarah's life made the thought of heaven very appealing. A place free from carpool responsibilities, juggling too many people's schedules, and no bills sounded a lot better than what she was looking at today. She had discovered God's love for her and knew he would only give her what she could handle. She just wished he didn't trust her so much. Trying to decrease distractions and do what was most important first sounded good in theory. Figuring out what should be the highest priority was hard in practice. She usually ended up responding to whoever was whining the loudest—adult or child.

She was so busy responding to her children's wants and needs that there was very little time to spend on the things that mattered in the long run. It was discouraging to see her kids' lack of interest in spiritual things. She felt guilty that she wasn't doing a better job of passing on her faith, but she just wasn't sure how to do it or when she could fit it in.

Overwhelmed by her schedule, Sarah felt that she wasn't doing anything well. There were too many evenings when she'd open the refrigerator door at five thirty hoping to be inspired, only to find that one essential ingredient that she needed for any recipe was either not in the house or was rock hard in the freezer.

She knew that she was giving her best to people outside her home and only had leftovers for her family. Most days she was too busy to pray. She was at her limit. Desperate to get a better grip on her life, she determined to make some changes and to get her priorities in order.

Can you relate to Sarah's situation? Have you reached that point where you recognize that something has to change? Take heart. You are not alone. Women today experience more opportunity, power, and freedom than ever before. With that liberation comes a plethora of choices that women one hundred years ago couldn't have imagined. It's hard to make the right choices, the ones that will lead to lives of lasting purpose. Living purposefully doesn't come naturally to most of us, but there are principles and practical solutions that can help even the most disorganized of us prioritize and live accordingly. When we open our hearts to God, he promises to "teach us to number our days aright, that we may gain wisdom of heart." (Psalm 90:12) A wise heart will help us to identify our priorities. Once they are identified, we'll have a better idea of what should be done first, most often, or not at all. They will help us to recognize the activities that we need to say no to.

I'd like to share with you the seven priorities that I have found to be most important in my life. Balancing my roles as a wife and mother of seven while doing a great deal of work outside my home is a challenge. I don't claim to have it all together. If you were to give me a complicated system for ordering my world, I'd probably be very inspired but would have trouble implementing it. If it's going to work in my life it has to be simple. It has to be something that I can remember while I'm in the middle of other tasks. Years ago, I discovered a business principle that has served me well in my personal life. It's called the $25,000 Planning Principle. Putting this lesson into practice has been the key to my remaining focused on what is most important.

THE $25,000 LESSON

In the early 1900's, Ivy Lee, a management consultant, was approached by Charles M. Schwab, the president of Bethlehem Steel. Schwab challenged Lee to show him a way to be more productive—to get more things done in the day. He promised to pay Lee anything (within reason) if it worked. Lee gave Schwab a blank piece of paper.

"Write down the things you have to do tomorrow," he said. Schwab wrote. "Now number these items in the order of their real importance," Lee continued. Schwab did it. "The first thing tomorrow morning," Lee instructed, "start working on number one and stay with it until it is completed. Next take number two and don't go any further until it is completed. Then proceed to number three, and so on. If you can't complete everything on schedule, don't worry. At least you will have taken care of the most important things before getting distracted by items of lesser consequence. The secret is to do this daily," continued Lee. "Evaluate the relative importance of the things you have to get done . . . establish priorities . . . record your plan of action . . . and stick to it. Do this every working day. After you have convinced yourself of the value of this system, have your men try it. Test it as long as you like. Then send me a check for whatever you think the idea is worth." Clearly, it made an enormous difference, because a few weeks later, Charles Schwab sent Ivy Lee a check for twenty-five thousand dollars. It was the most helpful and profitable principle he had ever learned in his business career."[12]

Once I figured out what was the most important priority in my life and listed the other key ones in order, I was better equipped for decision making. The use of my time improved greatly, and my heart was filled with peace. When things started to feel out of control, I could check my behavior against my priorities and see where I'd gone wrong.

As I approach any day and the many things I need to get done, I determine which task corresponds to which priority. I then put them on my list in order of importance *according to my priorities.* To the best of my ability, I do the things first that matter most in the long run. There are many reasons to choose one task over another. I can be led by my emotions (What do I feel like doing today?), by other people's expectations of me (I'd better do XYZ so no one is irritated with me), by whatever will give me short-term gain (I'm going to do the laundry because the pile is insanely high instead of having a heart-to-heart with my needy daughter). I wish I could say that I never do the wrong things first, but that would be a lie; one of my many children would take great delight in pointing out the truth. But this is my game plan, and I've found no better plan to help me stay on track.

At the end of my life, I want to look back and know that I poured my time and heart into the people and things that will matter in the long run. I want to live smart and healthy. I know that you do, too. So let's look at these seven priorities, one by one.

YOUR RELATIONSHIP WITH GOD

God first. With just two words, you may already be feeling that I'm suggesting something impossible to incorporate into your everyday life. But you picked up this book, so I'm going to assume that there is something within you that desires to give God that important place in your heart and life. We understand and believe that this is important, but how do we put it into actual practice?

Many things get in the way of putting God first. Sometimes we see the spiritual life as something so complicated that we feel defeated before we even begin. Other times we struggle to trust God. Disappointments in life can cause us to wonder if God is really for us. We get tired and weary, and it seems like far too much effort to add anything more to our plates, even if it's something good. Perhaps we are running at a hectic pace and are finding that all our time is being consumed with responding to the non-stop needs around us.

Let's get real. It isn't easy to put God first. But when we do, our hearts are centered, and everything else falls in place.

Queen Elizabeth I asked a man to travel abroad to attend to an important matter for her. "I sincerely wish I could, but I can't," he said. "My business is very demanding. It would really suffer if I left."

She replied, "Sir, if you will attend to my business, I will take care of *your* business."

Our King makes us the same promise: "Seek first the kingdom of God and his righteousness and all the other things shall be given you besides."[13]

OBSTACLES TO PUTTING GOD FIRST

Years ago, I worked as a waitress. I remember one of the most important things I had to learn at the beginning was how to lift and balance a large tray filled with all the plates of food. I had to get it up and over my shoulder, which I always found a little challenging. If I had my hand a little too far to the left or right, the whole tray would come crashing down. I needed to keep my hand right in the center in order to balance everything.

That is the place God needs to have in our lives. When he is at the center, everything else stays in balance. When we let other things take center stage, life comes crashing down. Putting God first doesn't just make him happy. It makes life work.

Putting God first may sound great in theory, but in reality it is challenging. Yet God never asks something of us that he doesn't give us the ability to accomplish. We need to move beyond putting God first in theory and put him there in practice, in the midst of the messiness of every day. How do we do this? How do we put God first when our experience of him has felt like nothing more than a list of rules to follow? What if we don't know if we trust him? And what of the times that we are tired and weary? Or when life has handed us so many disappointments that we wonder where God was when things got so out of control? And we are busy—so, so busy—and we can't imagine adding one more thing to the calendar. How do we get over these obstacles?

OBSTACLE #1: "I DON'T NEED ANOTHER LIST OF RULES."

Have you ever had any of these thoughts? I'm tired of failing over and over again. I'm sure God is sick of me. He must get tired of the fact that I keep making the same mistakes, over and over.

His forgiveness must reach a limit.

What God has asked of me is just too much. I can't do it. A life of holiness must be meant for the saints, but not for me.

I'm sick and tired of trying so hard.

I want to give up.

For those of us who have felt overwhelmed by expectations and the steep path to holiness, the thought of putting God first, of making him our highest priority, probably isn't very appealing. We may equate it with being given a list of rules, many of which seem out of touch with reality and the world we live in.

But when we look at God in this way, we completely miss the way he wants to relate to us. What God wants is a relationship with each one of us that is best described as a love story. He wants our obedience to him to be motivated by a love for him and a desire to keep that relationship as intimate as possible. It's the difference between a father-daughter relationship and that of a master and slave.

To better understand what that relationship looks like, we can learn a lot from the teachings of Saint Thérèse of Lisieux. Saint Thérèse was a French Carmelite nun who lived in the late 1800s.

She died at the age of twenty-four, but not before she had left behind beautiful, hope-filled writings that taught many people just how refreshing a relationship with God can be.

Saint Thérèse did not introduce anything new. She spent countless hours in Scripture and simply shared what she found. She took truths that had already been divinely revealed and then emphasized how very important they were. What she taught was packed with the truths of our Catholic heritage. The simplicity of the faith that she laid out for us is so completely Catholic that Pope Pius XII said, "She rediscovered the Gospel itself, the very heart of the Gospel."[14]

If he is saying that she "rediscovered" it, then something must have been lost in the way our faith was being communicated. She called her doctrine "the little way of spiritual childhood," and it is based on complete and unshakable confidence in God's love for us, reflected in Matthew 18:3: "Unless you change and become like little children, you will never enter the kingdom of heaven."

When Saint Thérèse's book, *The Story of a Soul,* first became available, the truths it contained were like a healing balm for people who had become afraid of God. The impression that many had of God's standard of holiness was that he was a tyrant without mercy, someone who was just waiting for people to mess up so he could swoop down and condemn them.

Do you see the vestiges of this today? Perhaps you need her words of comfort. Perhaps you, like me, will be refreshed by seeing how simple the spiritual life can be. The relationship God desires to have with each of us is simple enough that even a child can possess it.

This is the faith that Saint Thérèse had in abundance. As I studied her life and writings, three aspects of her relationship with God stood out. Each one is the living out of a childlike quality that God desires to see in each one of us. First of all, he longs for us to respond to his love for us not with fear and distance, but by loving him back. Second, he delights in that love being expressed through confidence in him—believing that he can do what we cannot. Lastly, he wants us to acknowledge that we aren't in charge—he is—and to surrender our will to his.

When we look at religion as some*thing,* rather than some*one,* it's easy to look at God as a distant figure who simply parcels out rules and judgment. But our religion is all about a life-giving relationship with someone: Jesus Christ.

Have you ever wondered why God made people? Did he create us so that he'd get a little fan club—a remnant of people who could praise him for all eternity? Did he need us? No, because God in his perfect completeness doesn't need anything. He was never lonely. So why did he make us?

He shares the answer to this question in the Catholic Catechism No. 221: "God has revealed his innermost secret: God himself is an eternal exchange of love, Father, Son, and Holy Spirit, and he has destined us to share in that exchange."

This means that for all eternity, before people were ever created, there has been an exchange of love going on between God the Father, Jesus the Son, and the Holy Spirit. God wasn't lacking love before he created people. So why did he create us, especially when he knew how much it would cost him? When he knew it would cost him his only son?

In the words of Christopher West, "Because love wants to share itself. True love wants to expand its communion. All the hungers we have for love, for union, for happiness are given by

God to lead us to him. The difference between a saint and the greatest sinner is where they go to satisfy that hunger."[15]

God wanted to share his love with us, and for us to experience a relationship of intimacy, happiness, and fulfillment with him. Throughout Scripture, we see different descriptions of that relationship. He refers to himself as our father, and us as his children. He is described as the vine, and we are the ever-dependent branches. He is the loving, self-sacrificing shepherd, and we are his sheep. He is the bridegroom, and we are his bride.

Throughout the Bible, his love letter to us, he reminds us of how he feels toward us. Through the prophet Hosea, he promises us, "I will betroth you to me forever; I will betroth you to me in righteousness and justice, in steadfast love and in mercy. I will betroth you to me in faithfulness; and you shall know the Lord."[16] As many of us know from personal experience, people often disappoint. Those whom we most want to remain steadfast and faithful don't always stay true. We long for significant relationships that go below the surface, but we can feel that some people we love don't really let us in to know who they truly are. God is different. He promises steadfast, faithful love, and if we desire it, he promises that we can know him, intimately. He tells us in Jeremiah 31:3, "I have loved you with an everlasting love." No matter how bleak our circumstances might be, this love will never fail us.

Sometimes we ask for proof of that love. We might pray and ask God to give us a parking place, fix a relationship, or send some other kind of sunshine. And when he doesn't, we might think this is proof that he doesn't really love us. But we're looking for proof in the wrong place. Romans 5:8 tells us that God proved his love for us when Christ died on the cross. God showed his love for us by holding nothing back—by giving up what was most precious to him, his son.

Saint Thérèse's response to that love was to offer herself to Jesus as his bride. She begged to be allowed to enter the Carmelite Convent earlier than was typically allowed. At age fifteen, she took the veil. Eight days later, her cousin was married. Sometime later, this cousin was visiting Saint Thérèse, explaining to her all the love and care she lavished on her husband. Saint Thérèse thought, "It's not going to be said that a woman will do more for her husband, a *mere mortal,* than I will do for my beloved Jesus."[17] She wanted all that she did to be pleasing for the king of kings, who had chosen her for his bride. She composed a wedding invitation reflecting the joy of being the bride of Jesus.

ALMIGHTY GOD
Creator of Heaven and Earth
Supreme Sovereign of the Universe
And

THE MOST GLORIOUS VIRGIN MARY
Queen of the Court of Heaven
Announce to you the Spiritual Marriage of their august Son
JESUS

KING OF KINGS *and* LORD OF LORDS
With
Little Thérèse Martin
Now Princess and Lady of the Kingdoms of the Childhood of Jesus and His Passion, given to her as a dowry by her divine Spouse from which she holds her Titles of nobility **OF THE CHILD JESUS** *and* **OF THE HOLY FACE.**

It was not possible to invite you to the wedding feast held on the mountain of Carmel, September 8, 1890, as only the heavenly Court was admitted, but you are nevertheless invited to the At Home tomorrow, the Day of Eternity when Jesus, the Son of God, will come in the clouds of heaven to judge the living and the dead in the full splendor of His majesty.

The hour being uncertain, you are asked to hold yourself in readiness and to watch. [18]

Like most little girls, Thérèse wanted to be the princess in a fairy tale. She wanted to be romanced by her knight in shining armor. She figured out at a far younger age than most of us that there is no one who rescues quite like Jesus.

Her whole life was the living out of that love relationship with Jesus. To her, it was not an abstract relationship. She absolutely adored him. She understood how God wanted all of us to respond to his love. What does God desire most from us? To be loved in return.

When I married my husband, it was because I loved him. Because I loved him, I preferred him, and I chose him above all others. Jesus wants to be chosen, to be preferred. To be loved.

The childlike faith that responds to God's love by loving him in return is living a modern-day fairy tale. It means loving God back, and becoming a princess in the bargain.

OBSTACLE #2: "I DON'T KNOW IF I CAN TRUST HIM."

How do we show Jesus our love? By having confidence in him.

It's so easy to shift from confidence in God to confidence in ourselves. We do this whenever we find ourselves white-knuckling in the spiritual life—trying so hard to be perfect that we are worn out. When this happens, we have forgotten the secret of the Christian life. God wants to do the work in us; he doesn't want our exhausted effort stemming from a belief that it all depends on us. This perspective ignores the indwelling Holy Spirit, as if that unbelievable gift makes no difference in our lives.

When Saint Thérèse was fifteen years old, she said that she wanted to be a saint. That was her lifelong goal. Is it yours? As she compared herself with the saints, though, she observed such a difference between her level of holiness and that of the saints. She described it as the difference between "a mountain whose summit is lost in the heavens and an obscure grain of sand, trampled under the feet of passersby." But instead of becoming discouraged, she wrote this:

> The good God would not inspire unattainable desires; I can then, in spite of my littleness, aspire to sanctity. For me to become greater is impossible; I must put up with myself just as I am with all my imperfections. But I wish to find the way to go to Heaven by a very straight, short, completely new little way. We are in a century of inventions: now one does not even have to take the trouble to climb the steps of a stairway; in the homes of the rich an elevator replaces them nicely. I, too, would like to find an elevator to lift me up to Jesus, for I am too little to climb the rough stairway of perfection. So I have looked in the books of the saints for a sign of the elevator I long for, and I have read these words proceeding from the mouth of eternal Wisdom: "He that is a little one, let him turn to me." So I came, knowing that I had found what I was seeking, and wanting to know, O my God, what You would do with the little one who would answer Your call, and this is what I found:

"As one whom the mother caresses, so I will comfort you. You shall be carried at the breasts and upon the knees they shall caress you." Never have more tender words come to make my soul rejoice. The elevator which must raise me to the heavens is Your arms, O Jesus! For that I do not need to grow; on the contrary, I must necessarily remain small, become smaller and smaller. O my God, You have surpassed what I expected, and I want to sing Your mercies.[19]

This is what she discovered: We don't have to do it all on our own. It's not all up to us. What we can't do on our own, Jesus will do.

The more we recognize our own weaknesses, the more we are reflecting the beatitude "Blessed are the poor in spirit, for theirs is the Kingdom of God." (Matthew 5:3) We are acknowledging that we aren't perfect super-saints but instead are spiritual children who need God to pick up the pieces of our lives and do with us what we cannot. When we acknowledge this, God is delighted. Isaiah 57:15 tells us, "I live in a high and holy place, but also with the contrite and lowly of spirit, to revive the spirit of the lowly, and to revive the heart of the crushed." God promises to fill the hearts of the broken who sincerely seek his face.

Father Jean d'Elbee wrote a great prayer: "Jesus, repair what I have done badly; supply for what I have left undone."[20] And he will.

Recognizing our littleness before God keeps us humble— a state we should be in throughout eternity. Saint Thérèse said, "In the evening of my life I shall appear before You with empty hands, for I do not ask You to count my works. All our justices are stained in Your eyes. I want therefore to clothe myself in your own justice and receive from Your love the eternal possession of Yourself." [21]

These thoughts come straight from Scripture. In Isaiah 64:5, we read, "All our just deeds are like polluted rags." If we come to God thinking that we are going to be accepted by him based on our "good conduct," he will point out that our righteousness is nothing compared to his infinite holiness. God holds out a standard of holiness that is perfection—perfection in action as well as in motive. According to Romans 6:23, "The wages of sin is death." Not just major sin. Any sin. This means that even a good deed performed with ill motive is enough to separate us from God for eternity. As Saint Thérèse said, "All our justices are stained in your eyes."

If that were the end of the story, we would be facing a very dismal, hopeless future. But Romans 6:23 goes on to say, "But the gift of God is eternal life in Christ Jesus our Lord." It is a free, undeserved gift of grace that God offers to us. He knew that we would fail, and that something would need to fill the gap between our best efforts at holiness and his standard of perfection. His solution wasn't some*thing*. It was some*one*—his perfect, sinless son, Jesus.

Saint Thérèse recognized that her solution to her hopeless state was nothing other than the Gospel. She said that if her justices or righteous deeds were stained, then she wanted to clothe herself in Christ's own justice. We see this described in 2 Corinthians 5:21: "For our sake, [God] made him to be sin who knew no sin, so that in him we might become the righteousness of God." This is the divine exchange—our sin for his righteousness.

How did God make him who had no sin to be sin for us? This was foretold by the prophet Isaiah: "But he was pierced for our sins, crushed for our iniquities; He bore the punishment that makes us whole, by his wounds we were healed." (Isaiah 53:5) Jesus accomplished this on the cross. Now all the merits of Jesus are ours. He fills our empty hands and hearts with his own virtues.

Yes, we are little. Yes, we are weak. Yes, we do fail, often. But God looks at our heart, and he sees our desire to trust him, to please him, to obey him. And he will make up where we are lacking, if we ask him.

God desires that we be like a child—confident in her father. He is our Heavenly Father, and when life feels like it's just too much, he wants us to crawl into his lap, holding all our cares and concerns, trusting that he is going to take care of everything.

This should be a great comfort to us when we feel at the end of our resources. Have you ever gotten to that point? I have, and it was there that I found him faithful to his every word and promise.

My oasis from the busyness of life is Camden, Maine, where the air is cool, the beauty of nature surrounds us, and the biggest thing we have to decide is what time we'll go to the library or out on the boat.

When we arrived one summer, I felt in desperate need of some time of refreshment. Morning after morning, I woke up feeling a familiar nausea. A pregnancy test (actually, three tests) confirmed that life wasn't going to get simpler. We had six children at the time, and my morning sickness and exhaustion made the thought of a seventh child feel overwhelming.

I would love to say that trusting God in this area of my life has come easily to me, but the truth is, it's one of the hardest. He has shown me, time and time again, that I need to trust him with my fertility, but all sorts of fears rise up in my heart when I'm faced with this path of obedience. I want to give each of my children what they need, and I wonder how I can do that when I'm stretched too thin. I don't want to gain weight. I get tired.

The laundry piles in my house can be insane. Added to this, I care about what people think, and know that many question our decision to be open to more children, or more heartaches through miscarriage. I've had three miscarriages, and the fear of going through that again gets the better of me.

Within days of the positive pregnancy test, something happened that really brought me to my knees—literally. And not because I was praying. The stomach flu hit our house with a vengeance, going from person to person and lasting a week. After our recovery, we cleaned the house with industrial-strength turbo-cleaner. My sister and her family arrived, and the house was filled with seventeen people. The stomach flu came back, and it hit every one of us. Again. And let me tell you, there are better ways to lose weight.

The obedience God had asked of me was feeling like a burden. And the stomach flu on top of pregnancy nausea? I couldn't take it anymore. My heart was heavy, and I was tired. When I crawled into bed each night, so weak and weary, I thought of Saint Thérèse and the elevator she used to draw close to God—Jesus's arms. I climbed into my Heavenly Father's lap in my prayer. I imagined picking up each of the things I was concerned about, each of the people I wanted to help but was unable to. As I held all these loved ones and concerns, I rested my head on his shoulder, and asked him to take care of it all.

Down in the pit, this is what I learned: I can't fix it all, but I am confident that he can. He might allow circumstances in my life that could make me wonder if he is asleep on the job. When this happens, God is seeing how far he can push my confidence. Will I still believe that he loves me? Will I still believe that he is in control? A childlike faith remains confident, even when the storms of life are rocking the boat.

And sometimes, he gives consolation in the midst of the storm. I think these comforts are little things he sends us to remind us that it's all going to be OK. One night, after a discussion about how hard it is for a mother of many to give her children all they need, I crawled into bed and cried, certain that I would fail in this incredibly important area of my life.

Up the stairs came my oldest, seventeen year old, Amy. "Mom," she said, "when can I make dinner for us this week? And I want to help with dinner when we get back home, too."

"Oh, Amy . . . you don't need to do that," I said. What I was thinking was that this was proof that I couldn't get it together. She recognized that the meals on the table had been rather pathetic since my morning sickness had started. . . .

"No, really," she said, "I want to. I love cooking."

I asked her if she was wondering why I was resting so much. She smiled and said, "Of course. I've seen this quite a few times before. Congratulations!"

And then I asked her the question that held all my fears. Afraid of her response, I whispered, "Have I been enough?"

She smiled and replied, "I love being from a big family. Of course there are times when you can't do everything. But there are things we learn because there are so many of us—and that's good for us. And I'm here to help when you don't have time for things."

I looked at my unselfish daughter, at her ability to set her own needs aside to help other people. I know she doesn't think the world revolves around her. This is an unusual trait in a teenager.

46

I think Amy can do anything she sets her mind to. If I could have, I would have met her every need. I would have made her lunch every morning. I would have always been the room mother and I would have thrown the best parties. Amy's hair bows would always have matched her outfits, and I would have sewn all her Halloween costumes. I would have given her all I could think of to make her happy. *If I could have.* But I couldn't.

But God knew what was best. The very limitations he has placed on me have helped her to be molded into a young woman I respect, love, and rely upon.

It took some time, but God brought me to a place where my fears subsided. One morning, I looked at my husband and said, "Today is the first day that I really think we are going to have this baby. And I feel like it's all going to be OK. I'm finally excited!" Then we loaded up the cars and began the long drive home from Maine. Leo took half the children in his car, and I had the other half in mine. Our spirits were high as we set out, but along the way, I started showing signs of miscarrying. I quietly shared this with Amy, who pulled out her iPod and asked me to listen to a talk she had heard at her Life Teen Leadership Conference that summer. It was given by Steve Allgeyer and was based on a children's book, *Harold and the Purple Crayon.*

In this book, Harold has a magical possession, a purple crayon. Anything that he draws comes to life. So if Harold wanted a car, he'd just draw it, and it would be real. If he wanted a lollipop, he'd only need to draw it, and it would be in his hand. Steve asked his listeners to think about what sort of thing they would draw if they had a magical crayon like that one.

It made me think. First of all, I figured I'd draw a perfect husband who said things like, "You look as young, thin, and

47

beautiful as the day I met you," when I'm pregnant and have just woken up. "Your work today has been intense, I know. So many demands are placed on you! Let me take care of dinner. Let me run you a bubble bath. Let me put the kids to bed." He would think I was perfect, even when I wasn't. He would know what I was thinking, without my needing to say it. He'd meet my every need, without my even asking.

Then I'd draw ever-grateful children who never left messes. They'd say things like, "Mom, thank you for everything you do for me. I see all your quiet sacrifices. Thank you for every sock you fold and every meal you make. Thank you for my brothers and sisters. They are the greatest gift you've ever given me. They never annoy me. I just love them. Thank you for your correction—I know you're just trying to help me to be the best person I can be."

And then I'd draw my house. It would be free of clutter. I'd have a mudroom with a place for everything, and everything in its place. There would be no laundry. It would look straight out of a magazine all the time, and would smell like baking bread and cinnamon. Fresh flowers would grace every room.

What life would you draw with your purple crayon? Deep down, isn't this what we want in life? We want to hold the purple crayon, and create the best circumstances possible. So we work, and we plan, and we do all that we can to achieve a life as close to our ideal as we possibly can.

And God looks at us, and he asks us to hand him our purple crayon.

Hand him the purple crayon? That's crazy! Because who knows what he might draw! He might draw suffering, or circumstances that we don't like. It's true that he loves us just as we are, but he also loves us too much to let us remain that way. And we know that he often chooses to allow experiences in our lives that are meant to grow us in holiness. But the process hurts, and we don't want the suffering. So we hold on tightly to our purple crayons. We might get up the confidence to hand it over for a little while, but when things become difficult, the temptation to snatch the crayon back is strong.

But as you look back on your life, can't you see that it's the times that God was drawing the picture that it turned out most beautifully? Sometimes it involved pain, but he always brings it all together in the end. The Creator of the Universe draws the most beautiful pictures, and as the Author of Life, he writes a better story than we ever could.

A child knows that she is not the one in charge. Children aren't typically the ones who decide where the family goes on vacation, what time is bedtime, and what is for dinner. There's a lot that a child just needs to accept and surrender to. A child is likely to surrender the purple crayon pretty easily. She doesn't really have much of a choice.

But as women, we *do* have a choice. Giving up the crayon is an act of love that means so much to God, because he knows how difficult it is. That is how we show our love. That is how we show our confidence in him. We surrender the purple crayon.

As Amy and I drove down the freeway, I thought about what I had heard. I offered God my purple crayon, yet prayed that he'd draw a happy ending to my pregnancy. Surrendering the purple crayon doesn't mean that we cease to have an opinion. It doesn't mean that we allow all our hopes to die. It means that we say "yes" to whatever God would choose to be best, even if it isn't what we want.

When I prayed, I know that God heard me. I also know that he saw my desire to be generous and free with my love. God's ways are not my ways, and his thoughts are not my thoughts. They are *greater* than my thoughts and ways.[22] With his ability to see beyond the present, to choose what would truly be best for me from an eternal perspective, God chose to say no to my prayer. And the loss of that baby was sad and painful.

In the days and weeks following my miscarriage, I had to continue to offer God my purple crayon. When I offered it, I was really offering up my need to understand exactly why God allows what he allows. I was offering him my trust, instead of allowing the root of bitterness to take hold in my heart. I offered him my weakness, when I really preferred offering him my strength. My prayers during that time weren't with eloquent words. Often, my prayer was simply standing in the shower, with my empty hands held out. "This is what I can offer you today, Lord," I would pray. "It's my emptiness. It's my hurt. It's the void that I feel in my heart. I wish I was offering you amazing works of service or perfectly executed plans. But all you really want is my heart. So here it is. Weak, imperfect, but yours."

When someone asked Saint Thérèse to summarize her childlike way, she answered, "It is to be disturbed by nothing." It is to hand over the purple crayon without fear and without reservation.

In the words of Archbishop Fulton Sheen, "We have to offer ourselves as pencils. Let Him write poetry. Let Him write prose. Let Him scribble. What difference does it make? This is happiness."[23]

The childlike faith that God desires to see in each one of us responds to his love by loving him back, proves that love through confidence in God, and accepts that God is the one in control. All these qualities can be found in these words from Saint Thérèse:

> I desire neither suffering nor death, yet I love both; but it is love alone which attracts me. Now it is abandonment alone which guides me. I have no other compass. My heart is full of the will of Jesus. Ah, if my soul were not already filled with His will, if it had to be filled by the feelings of joy and sadness which follow each other so quickly, it would be a tide of very bitter sorrow. But these alternatives do nothing but brush across my soul. I always remain in a profound peace which nothing can trouble. If the Lord offered me the choice, I would not choose anything: I want nothing but what He wants. It is what He does that I love. I acknowledge that it took me a long time to bring myself to this degree of abandonment. Now I have reached it, for the Lord took me and put me there.[24]

But how do you give your purple crayon to God if you don't know if you can trust him? That's a fair question. If you have ever been hurt or betrayed by someone, you know firsthand how difficult it is to give that person access to your heart. When we don't trust someone, we close off our hearts as an act of self-protection.

And how can we trust someone we don't know? We teach this lesson to our children at an early age, telling them not to talk to strangers. We know that not everyone is worthy of our trust.

If we are ever going to trust God, it is essential that we get to know him. We need to know his character in order to determine if he is worthy of our trust. There is a big difference between getting to know God as he really is and getting to know him as we *think* he is. This was a real issue for the Pharisees. They were waiting for the Messiah, but they had certain preconceived notions of what he would be like. When Jesus came to earth, he didn't match up with their list. He wasn't who they were looking for. As a result, they didn't get to know him, and they certainly didn't trust him. They missed him altogether!

If we want to get to know God, we need to get to know Jesus Christ. Hebrews 1:3 says that Jesus "reflects the glory of God and bears the stamp of his nature." Jesus himself said, "Anyone who has seen me has seen the Father."25

That is one of the reasons that reading the Bible is so important, especially the Gospels. As we read the stories of Jesus's life, we begin to get to know him. We see how he relates to people, the things he considers most important, and how much he loves us. In order to grow in our trust of God, it is essential that we believe that he loves us and wants what is best for us. These two passages give us reason to believe: "I have loved you with an everlasting love; therefore I have continued my faithfulness to you," (Jeremiah 30:3) and "For I know the plans I have for you . . . plans to prosper you and not to harm you, plans to give you a hope and a future." (Jeremiah 29:11)

Getting to know God takes courage and determination. But at some point, you need to take a leap of faith. It's always a temptation to paddle to the edge of the wave, take one look, and then retreat to what we know, to what we can control. But having faith is believing in what we don't see, and without faith, no one can please God. Having faith means we trust God, even when we don't have satisfying answers to all our questions.

Eventually, we need to get out of the driver's seat of our lives and let God be the driver. As someone once observed, "If God is your copilot, you need to change seats!" We need to let him be the one in charge. Our faith and trust in him will grow as we do this. It isn't something that someone can teach us—we have to experience what it means to trust in God firsthand.

As Rick Warren said, "Everybody eventually surrenders to something or someone. If not to God, you will surrender to the opinions or expectations of others, to money, to resentment, to fear, or to your own pride, lusts, or ego. . . . When we completely surrender ourselves to Jesus, we discover that he is not a tyrant, but a savior; not a boss, but a brother; not a dictator but a friend."[26]

OBSTACLE #3: "I DON'T KNOW IF HE REALLY UNDERSTANDS HOW HARD MY LIFE IS."

Have you ever said to yourself, "I'm just too tired and weary to put God first"?

I know of no better example of a person being tired and weary than Blessed Teresa of Calcutta. Mother Teresa worked tirelessly, day after day, and the minute she helped one poverty-stricken, ill person, there was another to take his place. The weariness must have been overwhelming. And in the midst of it all, she did not feel God's presence. She wrote letters to spiritual directors that reveal that she experienced profound loneliness, doubt, and abandonment. The fact that she continued to serve, despite not feeling the pleasure and comfort of God's presence, reveals she was a true example of a deeply mature follower of Christ. She was someone who put Christ first even when she didn't feel emotion about him. In spite of feeling a heaviness, a weariness, and doubt, Mother Teresa got up every morning and served her God. She did not rely on her emotions to determine what she should do. She knew what God had asked her to do each day, and what she did, she did for Jesus. She lived out Matthew 25:20: "Whatever you did for one of the least of these brothers of mine, you did for me."

We aren't all called to walk the same path as Mother Teresa, but we all have experienced times when we have felt devoid of spiritual emotion, when we've wondered if it all is worth it, when what we have been called to do seems to make little difference and never seems to end. It is at those times that we need to take a step back from our emotions and not overanalyze them. We need simply to focus on what has to be done at that very moment. Our emotions do not determine what is right or wrong. They should not determine our behavior.

Satan sees your weariness as a perfect opportunity to discourage you and tempt you to give up. He wants you to give in to despair. One of his most effective tactics is to whisper in your ear, "Is that all you are doing? What value does that have in the big scheme of things? You're just cleaning diapers and wiping noses and nursing sick kids." He will try to convince you that becauseyou aren't doing more, God isn't pleased with you. But nothing could be further from the truth.

God sees your circumstances. He understands better than anyone what you are dealing with. He sees the intentions of your heart. He sees your love for him and your desire to put him first.

God does not value you or love you because of what you do. Your dignity—your worth—does not depend on what you accomplish. Years ago, I was asked by a priest during spiritual direction, "What do you think of yourself?" I found it a very difficult question, and told him I could tell him what I figured other people thought about me. But that wasn't what he had asked. As I thought about his question, I realized that the words that came to my mind were "not good enough." As the words came out of my mouth, I was shocked. But I knew God loved me! I knew his love was unconditional. So why was there a striving in my heart, a sense that I needed to be better, I needed to be more, I needed to accomplish things in order to feel worthy of God's love?

This priest challenged me to renew my thinking every day. He encouraged me to begin each day in prayer, and to be reminded that God does not love me because of what I do. I do not have to be perfect to be worthy of God's love. And neither do you. You need to accept yourself as God sees you—as his beloved daughter. Your dignity does not come from what you accomplish or from what you do.

What God calls you to do, he does not expect you to do on your own strength. As Christians, we are filled with the Holy Spirit. It is as if we are a glove, empty and not much use on our own. But when we are filled with the Holy Spirit, he is like the hand filling the glove and doing the work through us. Do you feel empty and exhausted? Ask God to do the work through you. When you are able to get through yet another day, you will know that you have to give him the credit. It will increase your faith as you see him filling you with strength that is not your own it is his. Saint Paul wrote, "It is no longer I who live, but Christ lives in me."[27] Christ lives in you through the Holy Spirit. He will give you the strength and the endurance that you need for every task, for every day.

OBSTACLE #4: "I DON'T KNOW IF HIS PLAN IS REALLY THE BEST FOR ME."

Have you ever thought, "My life has not turned out the way that I wanted. And some small part of me blames God for that." If only we could go through life without expectations. We'd be so much better off! But that isn't the way we are wired. Before we are married, we think about how it will be when we find that special someone to spend our lives with. When we marry, we start to project what life will be like when we have children. We have children, and we start to focus on what it will be like when we finally have some free time again. The free time comes, and we look for something purposeful to fill our time. If life gets too busy or tiring, we look forward to retirement. Always looking forward. Always hoping life gets better or stays good. We never look forward and hope for suffering.

But life isn't predictable. Things don't turn out the way we have planned. We struggle with discontent. Infidelity, infertility, rebellious children, illness, death of loved ones, divorce, financial setbacks . . . all these things cause us to stand up and say, "Wait a minute, God, this isn't what I signed up for! This isn't the way it's supposed to work! If I'm doing what I'm supposed to be doing, why are you allowing things to get so messed up?!" We feel tempted to throw in the towel spiritually.

I remember well a period of time when my life wasn't what I thought it would be. Leo and I were living with our four children in Mexico. Leo traveled for work more often than he was home, and there were times I wasn't sure what country he was in. I was homeschooling the children, and had been dealing with a chronic illness for years that landed me in bed for about a week each month. My grandfather, who was one of the people I loved most in the world, was very ill, and I was flying to Minnesota to be with him whenever I could. In the midst of this, our yard became the playground for a pack of rats. While there is nothing like a rat infestation to motivate the children to close up the cereal boxes and Tupperware containers and potato chip bags in the pantry, overall, it's pretty much a nightmare.

Before you judge my housekeeping skills, allow me to place the blame for it all squarely at the doorstep of the Mafia. I'm not kidding. A Mexican Mafia boss owned the house two doors down from ours, and he was getting out of prison. The house hadn't been kept up while he was behind bars, but now that he was getting out, people had begun to clean things up. Basically, the rats left his house and came to ours. These rats were huge. They came in packs. They ran all over the kids' swing set and all over my patio and were not even slightly afraid of me. No matter how we poisoned them, they kept coming back. The last straw came the morning we found one in the oven.

In the midst of this, I decided to head to my parents' house a little early for Christmas. It was all too much. On the flight there, a woman on board died and we had to emergency land in Texas. I rented a car when we finally got to Dulles Airport, and got lost on the way to my parents'. I walked in the door, burst into tears, gave the kids to my parents, and went to bed. As I crawled into bed, I said a prayer: "Dear Lord, I am at my limit. This is not what I signed up for. I can't take any more. I am only asking one thing of you. All I ask is that you not take Papa home to be with you until after Christmas." I turned out the light to go to sleep, and the phone rang. It was my aunt, saying that Papa had just died. My first thought was, "God, did you NOT HEAR ME?! Was that too much to ask?! I told you I couldn't take any more!"

I learned some lessons in the aftermath of these experiences.

In John 11, we find the story of Mary, Martha, and Lazarus, three of Jesus's dearest friends. Lazarus was very ill, so Martha sent for Jesus, believing that if Jesus came, he could heal Lazarus, her brother. Of course Jesus would heal him! If he had healed countless strangers, he certainly would heal such a dear friend!

When word came to Jesus that Lazarus was ill, he responded in an unexpected way. He waited where he was for two more days. When Jesus finally arrived, he found that Lazarus had been dead and in the tomb for four days. We can imagine Martha's emotions as she saw Jesus. "If only you had been here, my brother would not have died!"

How did Jesus respond to the grief surrounding him? He was deeply moved in his spirit and troubled, and he wept. Jesus knew that he had the power to raise Lazarus from the dead; he knew how the story was going to end, yet his response was to cry. As Jesus looked at all the people mourning the loss of Lazarus, I wonder if he thought, "This is not how it was supposed to be. When I created the world, there was no death. I never intended for people to have to suffer as they do." I wonder if his heart was overwhelmed by the reality of what sin had done to the world he created and to the people in it?

When I was suffering with grief over my grandfather, Jesus was weeping alongside me. And he doesn't do this just for me. He weeps with all of us when we're suffering. When your marriage is failing, Jesus weeps with you. That is not how he created marriage to be. When you or your loved one are ill, Jesus weeps with you. He didn't intend for there to be sickness in the world. When your children rebel, Jesus weeps with you. His desire was that children grow to respect and honor their parents. All of these things came into the world as a result of sin. None of them were part of his creation. They came because of sin. He grieves alongside us.

And sometimes, when what we are dealing with is overwhelming, he scoops us up and carries us. We don't always realize this is what is happening. You might be familiar with the poem "Footprints." In it, a man dreams he is walking along the beach with the Lord. He notices that for most of the time, there are two sets of footprints in the sand. But during the very saddest and lowest times in his life, there is only one set of footprints. He doesn't understand why God would leave him when he needed him most. God responds by saying, "My son, my precious child, I love you and I would never leave you. During your times of trial and suffering, when you see only one set of footprints, it was then that I carried you."

God promises us that he will never give us more than we can endure. In 1 Corinthians 10:13 we are assured: "No temptation has seized you except what is common to man. And God is faithful; he will not let you be tempted beyond what you can bear. But when you are tempted, he will also provide a way out so that you can stand up under it."

When we are suffering, when life isn't turning out the way we have hoped, we are tempted to make God less than the first priority of our hearts. We are tempted to replace his priorities with our own. When he doesn't seem to be doing a very good job of looking after us, then we often take back control—we take back the purple crayon—we stop praying, and stop seeing life from God's perspective. We can even begin to think that God owes us the things that we long for. This is dangerous territory.

Instead of focusing on all of the good things that God has done for us and given us, we can develop hearts of ingratitude. We can easily fall into the trap of comparison, wishing that he had given to us what we can clearly see he has given to someone else.

We must never lose sight of the fact that we have no claim on God's mercy. He doesn't owe us! Our sins more than outweigh the good we've done. Because of my sin, what I *deserve* is death. But because of his great love for me, Jesus died in my place. How often do I think about that? If I'm honest, not often enough.

The mystery of ingratitude is that after all that God has given us, we still expect more. Imagine if someone saved your life and then you spent the rest of your life expecting him to give you more. It would be unthinkable! But that is what we so often do with Jesus. We do not give him the consideration and respect that we would give a mere man.

Even in the midst of suffering, we must never lose sight of all that God has given us. We must still put God first and remain loyal to him. We need to fight against doubt. We need to remember his goodness and his love, and all that he has given us.

OBSTACLE #5: "I DON'T KNOW IF HE UNDERSTANDS HOW BUSY I AM."

You might be thinking, "This sounds so much like the right thing to do, but how would I ever fit it in? Kicking it up a notch in my spiritual life would take so much time! I'm just too busy to add one more thing to my plate."

God sees all that you do, and he appreciates every sacrifice you make. Every time you get up with a sick child at night when you'd rather sleep, every time you set aside what you want to do in order to drive your child somewhere, every piece of laundry that you fold, each toy you pick up off the floor, the countless meals you make, the times that you set aside your needs to listen to a hurting friend, the meetings you attend and the things you organize, the hours spent at work to help provide for your family—he sees it all.

You are busy. In fact, "busy" might be an understatement for your life. You are constantly pulled by many people in many directions.

You may have children, and children always seem to need more than we are able to provide. You may have a husband who has high expectations of you. Are your parents or in-laws demanding? Do you find it hard to balance what they want from you with what you need to give your immediate family? You may have friends who are in need of more time than you feel able to give. Work may bring constant pressure, and the work-life balance may seem ever elusive. Do you ever feel that everyone wants a little piece of you, and pretty soon there's not going to be anything left to give?

In the book of Revelation, Jesus spoke through Saint John to the church in Ephesus. "I know your deeds," he said, "your hard work and your perseverance. . . . You have persevered and have endured hardships for my name, and have not grown weary. But I hold this against you: You have forsaken your first love."[28] He was talking about their love for him.

God whispers that same message to us in our busy, nonstop world. God doesn't say this to us because he just doesn't understand all that we have to do. Who more than Jesus understands what it feels like to be so busy and inundated with people's needs? God tells us that we need to go back to our first love, to him, so that he can begin to make sense and order out of the madness that is our lives. If we are willing to make him the first priority of our day, then he promises to come down in the midst of the craziness and start ordering things for us.

This is one of those things that you have to *do* in order to understand. Just as we learn to pray by praying (not by attending a seminar about prayer), we have to step out and put God first before we can experience and understand how he can create balance in the midst of our disorder.

Our prayer life is a direct measure of how well we are placing God first in our lives. If we are not praying, we are not making him a priority. Service *for* God is not a substitute for spending time *with* him. It is only through spending time in prayer that we will begin to see what things in our day are most important to God, and which things we can let go of. We are never going to get it all done, but we all want to get done the things that matter most. The problem is, it *all* seems important. Spending time with God helps us to see our lives through his perspective. Only God knows which of your commitments are most important. Perhaps God has gifted you with the ability to spin many plates. People around you may be telling you that you are doing too much. Maybe, maybe not. God knows what you can handle, and it may be that it is far more than the average person. But only through close communion with God will you know what things he wants you to focus on. Perhaps you do have too much on your plate, and you need to pare down some of your activities. God is the one who will help you to see clearly what needs to go, what should stay.

Finding time to pray is not an option. It must be the most protected part of your daily schedule. I highly recommend morning prayer time, as it sets the tone for the day. I could not accomplish anything in the way that God desires if I did not devote the first part of my morning to him. There are seasons in life when giving God the first part of the day is especially difficult. During those times, look for the first pocket of quiet in your day. Ask God to provide it for you. And when it comes, reserve it for God. Resist the temptation to throw in another load of laundry or answer just a few e-mails.

With seven children, there is little time during the day for me to sit quietly in prayer. Somehow, just knowing that I am attempting to be "off-limits" makes the smallest issue unbearable for my children. With all the best intentions in the world, it's hard to pray. God loves me no matter what I do or don't do, but I am believing an illusion if I think that my good intentions alone—the desires of my heart—somehow fix what happens when I don't give prayer the highest priority in my life.

I'd like to share with you some of the practical things that help me with my prayer life. I do not share them so that you will conclude I'm very devout. The truth of it is, I am very weak, and without prayer I am an entirely different person.

For me, making prayer happen starts the night before. Instead of watching TV in the evening, I try to do everything that can be done ahead of time for the morning. Making school lunches, laying out clothes, setting the table for breakfast, packing bags and leaving them by the door are all tasks that can be done the night before. When I do this, I wake up with a clear and focused mind. I'm not too distracted to pray. I then make sure that all the things I use during my prayer time—my journal, my Bible, and my rosary—are in the place where I pray. I always pray in the same place. This is my little sanctuary.

When I have done as much as I can the night before, I get to bed. This is so important, because I love my sleep. There are times I get less sleep because I have some deadlines to meet, but ideally, I try to be in bed by ten or ten thirty each night. I really believe that those hours before midnight are more beneficial to our bodies than the ones after midnight.

The alarm goes off early. After making my cup of tea, I'm ready for my prayer time. Lord forgive me, but I don't think I will ever give up tea for Lent. I just don't think it would be pretty.

This time in the morning is my prelude to the sacraments. It's what makes the sacraments more meaningful, because I've taken the time to prepare my heart before receiving them. The way in which I pray isn't a formula that will fit everyone's preferences or needs, but it's what works for me. It's what draws me closer to Christ, settles my heart, and gives me the focus I need for the day ahead. I share the steps I follow during this morning quiet time in that spirit, simply offering them as suggestions. If something appeals to you and you want to incorporate it into your prayer life, great! If not, that's fine, too. The important thing isn't that you follow a prescribed method; it's that you make the time to focus on God.

I start with a blank page in my journal, writing a quick note to God. "Dear Lord," the note begins, "This is what I need to confess," or "This is what I'm worried about," or "This is what I really need direction on," or "Thank you so much for coming through for me yesterday!" Whatever is in my heart, I get it out on paper. I then turn to the back of my journal for my daily prayers. I have go-to prayers written out, categorized by my priorities. My first page lists prayer requests about my relationship with God. Currently, I'm praying that he will:

* Help me to find my security and worth in him instead of in my accomplishments

* Guard me from being enslaved to my to-do list

* Help me to be fully present in the moment

* Free me from my perfectionist tendencies

* Help me to desire God's approval more than that of any person

* Guard my mouth—help me to speak wisely. (If I don't have anything nice to say, help me to say nothing at all.)

I also pray that I will always credit God with any good in me.

Next, I pray for my marriage. I pray for Leo's concerns, asking God from time to time to give me specific things I can pray about. I also ask him to help me:

* Listen well to Leo.

* Look for ways that I can help Leo on a daily basis instead of waiting for him to make my life easier.

* Spend wisely so I don't cause Leo to feel stressed financially.

* Protect our marriage from evil and emotional distance. Bind us together with cords that cannot be broken, with God at the center.

Then I pray for my children. I have monthly prayers (this is listed later, in the chapter on children), and I have specific requests for each child. Each year, Leo and I take a weekend to get away and set goals. We discuss the big picture of where we are in our marriage and how we're doing financially, and then analyze the kids in terms of their spiritual, physical, emotional, and academic development. We identify the main area of weakness for each child, and those become our prayers and parenting focus for the next year. So that is one aspect of my prayer for each child.

My next priority is my home, and so I pray about that, too. My current prayer is that my home will be filled with the unmistakable scent of Christ. May it be calm, not chaotic. May we be purposeful about family meals. Specifically, I pray that God will help me get the dinner made and on the table. I ask God to help my kids be consistent with their chores, and to help me be consistent about checking on them. I was told once not to expect what I don't inspect, and I find it really hard to remember to follow through on this. So I ask for God's help. Then I ask him to help all of us show our gratitude to him by caring for the lovely home he's blessed us with.

The next priority is my other relationships, outside my immediate family. I list the loved ones who are closest to my heart, and pray for their specific needs. This is also when I pray for a few special priests and other spiritual leaders who have greatly influenced my life. I pray for protection for them, for continued faithfulness and fruitfulness as they serve God so selflessly.

Lastly, I pray over the priority of outside activities. Walking with Purpose, the apostolate that fills me with passion and intention, is my focus at this point. I pray that God will be at the helm and the heart of it all. I pray that I will never lose sight that it's all about God—*about* him, *done by* him, and for him. I pray that God will draw women from all paths of life, and that hundreds of thousands will experience conversion of heart. I know this is a tall order, but I also know that this is the kind of prayer request that God loves to answer with a resounding YES, and that he can do anything. My final prayer is the one I pray as I prepare to write the Bible study material that we use for Walking with Purpose:

> Dear Lord,
> I am your instrument. All instruments have limitations.
> You can use anything—even things that are mediocre.
> It's your power, not mine. It's your wisdom, not mine.
> It's your creativity, not mine. I love and trust you. This work is not mine. It's yours. Use me as you see fit.

I then open my Bible and spend some time in Scripture. Sometimes I read the daily gospel reading, sometimes a Psalm and a proverb, sometimes a verse on a subject I'm struggling with. I'm not reading for intellectual growth. I'm reading prayerfully, asking God to transform me by his words.

I have come to love these mornings. I can honestly say that early morning is now my favorite time of day. No one interrupts me. There are no children's needs, no phone calls, no distractions.

You may not need to get up terribly early. The time on the clock is not what matters. What matters is that prayer is the highest of priorities in your life.

What is keeping you from making God the highest priority in your life? Have you thought he just wants you to follow rules, when what he really wants is your love? Have you struggled to trust him? Have you been weary? Have you been disappointed with what life has dealt you? Have you been too busy—loving God in your heart, but failing to love him in your schedule?

I challenge you to identify one thing that you feel is keeping you from allowing God to be the highest priority in your life. Instead of vowing "from now on I'll . . ." try to make a "for the next thirty days" promise.

If we attend to the things that are most important to God, he'll come into the mess of our lives and begin to create beauty and order. The purple crayon is safe in his hands, and he won't scribble. He'll create a masterpiece.

TENDING TO YOUR HEART

Because women are often the nurturers and caregivers in society, it is very easy for us to become adept at putting our needs on the back burner. Have you ever lost sleep in order to listen to a hurting friend? Have you taken on more responsibilities at work than you needed to in order to help someone who was overwhelmed? Have you ever been sick and really needed to go to the doctor, but heard yourself saying, "There are so many things I need to get done for the kids. I'll take some medicine and just keep going"? Have you given so much that your own needs have gone unmet? Are you skating on the thin ice of burnout?

During my senior year of college, I asked an older woman who was mentoring me the best way for me to stop being so self-centered. She told me to have children. A little more than a year later, I had embarked on that adventure, and found that kids definitely help us take our focus off ourselves. Much of that is good, but sometimes it can be to our detriment.

Sometimes we feel that we are running in circles. We multitask as never before, with e-mails, texts, and phone calls reaching us wherever we are. We are never unavailable. How often do you sit in quiet? Most evenings in my house we have my husband's jazz music playing on the stereo, someone's noise from the computer, one child practicing piano, another the recorder, and someone talking to me as I make dinner. I'm constantly thinking, "If we can't have one source of noise, can we at least have one source of music?"

I remember a few years ago going to a fitness assessment at a local athletic club. I sat down to be interviewed by a perky young blonde with a body that I hoped I could have by simply buying the gym membership, but unfortunately it seemed to have a lot to do with her hard work and genetics. She began the interview by asking my name, weight, height, and age. I did OK on the first three questions, but I drew a complete blank on my age. "Thirty-six," I said. "No, wait. Is it thirty-five?" I had to sit down and do the math while she looked at me as if I had completely lost my mind.

In this world of noise and busyness, it is hard for us to find the time to give ourselves even a little attention. But it's important that we do. Flying on an airplane, one of the first things we are told is that in case of an emergency, we are to put the oxygen mask on ourselves first. Then we'll be able to help others.

When you feel worn out, depleted, and in need of refreshment, what do most people recommend that you do? Go shopping! Take a nap! Try some exercise! Do something fun! Get a manicure! Take some vitamins! Go to a movie! Have some wine! I'm not saying that these are bad things. And the truth is, each one of those things can make us feel a little better—temporarily. But then the glow wears off, and we return to exactly the same place we were before. It's given us superficial relief, but it hasn't really helped us on a deeper, soul level. As a result, our souls remain parched and dry.

If we really want refreshment, if we want to refuel in a way that will truly sustain us, if we want to be filled up enough that we can pour into others, we need to go beyond the superficial. This is why Priority No. 2 is tending to our hearts. God doesn't want us to run ourselves ragged, only looking to the needs of others and never caring for ourselves. He wants us to live in a way that will deeply satisfy. In Proverbs 4:23 we read, "Above all else, guard your heart, for it is the wellspring of life."

What is meant by "the heart"? Our heart can be defined as the core of who we are. This is where our emotions are located. When we feel criticized, betrayed, or abandoned, the feelings come from here. When we feel like we're welling up with happiness, it's coming from the heart. When we feel love for someone, it pours out of the heart. It's what makes us distinct and unique.

What are some ways in which we attempt to guard our hearts? When we've been deeply hurt, our tendency is to put up barriers around them. We know what it feels like to be rejected or criticized or betrayed, and we close off our hearts in order to avoid the risk of someone hurting us again. We don't let anyone in. Our goal is self-sufficiency. We avoid intimacy. We rely on ourselves and determine that as long as we aren't vulnerable, we'll be safe.

Sometimes we harden our hearts through destructive habits. We might behave as if we don't care. We seek to escape from what we're feeling inside. We distract ourselves from feeling deeply or analyzing our needs and desires.

Where does this behavior come from? It can result from unconfessed sin, self-hatred, and guilt. We may question our worth or dignity, and as a result think that the way we treat our bodies doesn't matter. It can also begin with a hurt. It might be an experience of abuse or betrayal, growing up with alcoholic parents, the infidelity of a spouse, the loss of a loved one, or the pain of divorce.

If this hurt happened in childhood, its impact is often greater. This is because children don't *think* things as much as they *feel* things. Children perceive themselves as the center of the universe, and so very often they feel responsible for whatever has hurt them. Because of this, the hurt imprints on a child's personality.

This hurt can cause us to see ourselves as victims. In some cases, we can become defined by the hurt. The hurt becomes *who we are*. If we have allowed ourselves to be defined by the hurt, we will be filled with self-pity.

Very often, depression, an inability to forgive, an eating disorder, or sexual dysfunction will result.

A person defined by her hurt is often filled with a determinism that says, "I can't help how I react! Because I'm a victim, I'm allowed a certain amount of escapism. Because of _____, I deserve _____." This "deserved escapism" can be overeating, sex, alcohol, or destructive behavior.

These deserved escapes reveal an inner attitude that says, "I am not responsible. I am not responsible for the problem or what has resulted from it. I'm entitled to all these things. I know it's not good, but the world should make up for my hurt." There is no personal responsibility. The anger causes you to dwell on your hurt, and reminds you that you're a victim, and the cycle begins again. You dwell on the hurt, you define yourself by the hurt, you excuse your behavior, your behavior makes you feel worse, you're filled with anger, and around and around the cycle goes.

We may think we're protecting ourselves, but living this way actually hardens the heart. The heart becomes wary and guarded, and not in the way that God desires. God knows that the essence of who we are is going to well up from our hearts. Because of this, he wants us to allow him to be the guardian of our souls. He longs for us to offer him our hearts, so that he can fill us, heal us, tenderly love us, forgive us, and lead us to a place of restoration. When we surrender our hearts to his care, he promises to guard them.

God knows the questions we hold deep in our hearts. We want to know if we are of value. We need to hear that we are loved. We wonder how far that love will go. Is it conditional? Does it have a limit? We want someone to think we are worth so much that we are worthy of sacrifice. We hope to have someone by our side who will go to the hard places with us, who won't abandon us when we are unlovable or fail to measure up to expectations.

God longs to enter the deepest parts of our souls and meet the most profound of these needs.

But many of us conclude that who we really are isn't worth all that much. Perhaps we were given that message in childhood, or in adult relationships. We may even have people in our lives who say they love us, but we worry that if they really knew us, deep down, then they wouldn't love us. So we push the desire to be loved away, assuming that being loved is reserved for those who have it all together. Many of us are in a constant state of striving, thinking that perhaps we just need to try harder.

In order for God to answer our questions, we need to recognize how we define our worth. How do we define ourselves? We may first think of the roles we play: mother, wife, daughter, friend.

When we define ourselves by our roles, we can get into trouble. For example, many women define themselves by their roles as mothers, and at times allow their children's successes and failures to be their own. Nowhere is this clearer than on the sidelines of kids' sporting events. I believe that the vocation of mothering is one of the most important in the world, but being a good mother does not mean that who your child is and what your child does should define you. There needs to be a healthy separation of mother and child, one that lets the child be who he or she is, and prepares the mother for the inevitable day when that child will leave the home.

A friend shared her experience at a conference she attended in conjunction with her work. In a small group exercise each participant was asked to introduce him- or herself without any reference to job or occupation. As the conversation moved around the circle toward her place, she had to admit she wasn't sure what to say. She had allowed her job to define her almost exclusively.

Defining ourselves by our roles isn't our only pitfall. We can also fall into the trap of defining ourselves by what we accomplish. Imagine being injured in an accident that costs you the ability to do the things you most enjoy or the things that take up most of your time. Would you feel that who you were had changed? Do you feel that your value as a person depends on what you produce? Do you feel that you could always be doing more, or doing things a little better? Does your self-esteem come from your work? Are you afraid of failing? Do you struggle with perfectionism? If so, this is a strong indication that you are defined by what you do.

We can also define ourselves by what people think of us. How others think of us can become our mirror. When this is our struggle, we often find that we do things in order to be praised and to be noticed. Our reputation is incredibly important to us. We want to be accepted, to fit in—this is our motivation. At times, it becomes an obstacle in our desire to please God. Spiritual writers call this "human respect," meaning you care so much about making sure other people respect you that you betray your own conscience.

An example of this is found in Matthew 14. King Herod placed a high premium on what people thought of him. Saving face and protecting his reputation had far-reaching consequences, harming not just himself but also innocent people in his path. John the Baptist had condemned Herod for marrying his brother's wife, and so Herod had John imprisoned. In a moment of passion, Herod made an imprudent commitment and told his wife's daughter that because of her beautiful dance in front of his courtiers, she could ask for anything and he would grant it. She, at her mother's request, asked for the head of John the Baptist on a platter. Herod had a choice: He could do the right thing and not take the life of an innocent man, or he could save face and deliver on the girl's horrific request. Herod ended up perpetrating a despicable crime (executing a man he knew was innocent) just to avoid being ridiculed by his courtiers.

King Herod presents an extreme example of where we can end up when we value others' opinions more than God's. We might read his story and excuse ourselves by saying, "What harm is there in my little compromises?" When we justify our actions, we are ignoring the harm we do to ourselves when we feed on the approval of others instead of the deeply satisfying, unconditional love of God.

This approval seeking can begin in childhood and become an ingrained habit by adulthood. One of my favorite books to read to my children is *You Are Special,* by Max Lucado. I just read it the other night to my son, Jonathan, who gave himself a very unusual haircut and then was afraid to go to school in case people teased him.

This story is about a group of wooden people called the Wemmicks. The Wemmicks all had two boxes; one contained golden stars, and the other, gray dots. They spent their entire day walking around and giving one another either stars or dots. The Wemmicks who were pretty and didn't have scratches on their wood were given stars. The ugly ones were given dots. Stars were earned for being talented and for knowing big words. Punchinello was one of the Wemmicks who got a lot of dots. He tried to jump high, but he always fell. And when he fell, he'd be given a dot. Sometimes falling scratched his paint, so he got another dot for that. He got so many dots that Wemmicks started giving him dots for no reason at all. They would say that he deserved all those dots, that he wasn't a good Wemmick. Punchinello agree with them, and began to spend time with other Wemmicks who had a lot of dots. He felt better around them.

One day, Punchinello met a Wemmick who was different from any other he had ever seen. She didn't have any dots or stars. Sometimes people would come up to her and try to put a star or a dot on her, but they would just fall off. Punchinello was amazed, and asked her why the dots and stars didn't stick. "It's easy," she said. "Every day I go see Eli. Why don't you go and see him? Go find out for yourself."

Punchinello was afraid that Eli wouldn't want to see him, but he finally mustered enough courage to go to Eli's workshop. When he entered the workshop, he heard a deep, strong voice call his name. "Punchinello?"

"How do you know my name?" asked Punchinello. Eli told him that of course he knew his name—he had *made* Punchinello. Eli stooped down and picked him up. He noticed all of the dots on his body and commented on them. "I didn't mean to get all of those bad marks," Punchinello said.

"Oh, you don't have to defend yourself to me, child. I don't care what the other Wemmicks think. You shouldn't either. Who are they to give stars or dots? They're Wemmicks, just like you. What they think doesn't matter, Punchinello. All that matters is what I think. And I think you are pretty special."

Punchinello laughed. "Me, special? Why? I can't walk fast. I can't jump. My paint is peeling. Why do I matter to you?"

Eli looked at Punchinello, put his hands on those small wooden shoulders, and spoke very slowly. "Because you're mine. That's why you matter to me. . . . The stickers don't stick on your friend because she has decided that what I think is more important than what they think. The stickers only stick if you let them. The more you trust my love, the less you care about their stickers. You are special because I made you. And I don't make mistakes."[29]

It's just a children's story, but the message is one that many of us need to hear. We decide whether or not other people's opinions are going to matter, and the more we struggle in this area, the more time we need to be spending with our Creator. Defining our worth by other people's opinions of us is a pitfall we want to avoid.

Another area in which many of us struggle is defining ourselves by our possessions. John Paul II talked a lot about how we are a society that is based more on having than on being. If all that you owned were taken away, would you be a different person? Do you need things in order to feel good about yourself? Is your worth tied to the clothes you wear, the car you drive, or the house you live in? Do you struggle with being content? Do you long for the gifts that you can see God giving to others?

God gives us gifts to know him, love him, and serve him so we can spend eternity with him in heaven. All we have been given is to be used for that purpose. But we have a choice: We can use what God has given us to know, love, and serve *ourselves*. We can make an idol of money or possessions. We can look to these things to make us feel more secure. But because these things aren't guaranteed to last, we actually become insecure. This is a disordered attachment to the things of the world because God is not in the equation, giving us our dignity and security.

With each of these ways of defining ourselves (by what we do, by what others think of us, by what we possess), we are at the center. Our dignity and sense of worth will always be in danger if we live with ourselves at the center. Why? Because we are counting on externals that are always out of our control.

We can become sick and therefore unable to produce anything. Others can criticize us. We can lose all we possess. And if that happens, we think we will cease to be lovely and worthwhile.

Until we come to a place where we stop defining ourselves in these ways, we will always struggle with our sense of worth. We won't live in the freedom that comes from knowing we are unconditionally loved.

So what is the solution to this dilemma?

We need to get out of the center of our lives, and put God there. Our dignity, our true identity must come from being God's precious, beloved daughters. If we live as God's beloved daughters, then all that we do will be done for God. Instead of pursuing accomplishments for a sense of worth, we'll do what we do in order to know, love, and serve God better.

If we live as God's beloved daughters, then we'll fill up our hearts with his unconditional love each morning. This will help us go into our days ready to love and give to people rather than needing them to love us so we feel good about ourselves.

If we live as God's beloved daughters, then we'll recognize that all we have is from God, and really belongs to him. He entrusts things to us to take care of them, and to use them for his purposes. We'll want to use all we have for him. We'll always live with the awareness that what we possess is a gift from God, our loving father. He wants us to enjoy these things as gifts, but as far as our identity and sense of worth goes, he wants that to be defined by our relationship with him as his daughters.

No matter how strong we are, we all need to know that we are loved. God created us that way! He is the one who placed that desire in our hearts. So when we long for someone to celebrate us, to protect us, to be captivated by us, that's a God-given desire.

God's desire was for your first taste of that kind of love to come from your dad. He wanted you to be loved so beautifully that it wouldn't be hard for you to understand that your Heavenly Father is absolutely crazy about you. He wanted your father's love to be a model of God's love for you. But for many of us, this isn't what we experienced. Some of us were neglected by our fathers, which delivered the message "You are unimportant." Some of us had distant or absent fathers due to death, divorce, or alcoholism. This delivered the message "You can't count on anyone to be there for you." Some of us have been mentally, physically, or sexually abused by our fathers. This has left us with the sense that we aren't worthy—we're dirty, stained, used goods. Some of us never felt our father's blessing or sense of approval. This has left many of us listening to an inner voice that says, "You aren't good enough."

A father's wound hits us in the deepest part of our hearts, the part that defines who we are and what we are worth. As a result of this, we can struggle with low self-esteem and deep emotional pain. In order to feel better about ourselves, some of us focus on our appearances or performances, and some of us don't bother at all, figuring we'll never be good enough, so why even try? We can struggle with feelings of unworthiness and incompetence. Some of us turn to harmful addictions to try to ease the pain. It's hard to trust. We convince ourselves that if we don't trust anyone, if we don't hope, then no one can let us down.

How this must deeply grieve God. This is not how he wanted us to be treated. This is the result of sin's entrance into the world, and it has destroyed and damaged too many of God's precious daughters. When God sees this happen, it breaks his heart.

God also understands who the real enemy is. He recognizes that when he gave man the gift of free will, some people would choose to reject him. In doing this, a cycle of hurt began. If we were to look at the ways in which our parents were parented, we would recognize that they have parented us from a place of brokenness. They have their own hurts and needs. This doesn't excuse sin, but it reminds us that the source of our pain goes back to the Garden of Eden and the entrance of sin into the world.

You may have felt alone in your pain, but God never left your side. He was always there. He saw what you endured. He cried alongside you. He longs to redeem and restore all that was lost through your hurtful circumstances. The very things that the enemy of your soul wants to use to defeat you, God wants to bring good from. He wants to see you healed and free. And he has the unlimited power to do it.

God absolutely adores you. In John 15:16, Jesus affirmed this truth when he said, "You didn't choose me. I chose you." The prophet Jeremiah reminded us, "Before [God] formed you in the womb, [he] knew you."[30] God chose you to be his princess before you were born. God is the king of the universe, and so, because you are his daughter, you are royalty. You have an important role to play in his kingdom. Even when you were in your mother's womb, God had important works that he chose for you to do. He chose for you to be born in this place, in this particular generation, so that you could step out and fulfill your unique purpose. He has chosen you to do something special that only you can do. He has amazing plans for you. He knows you deeply, which means that he understand your failings, your inadequacies, and your past mistakes. But he also sees your gifts and your potential. He knows that your efforts combined with his supernatural grace are enough to move mountains and change the world.

There is nothing that God wouldn't do for you. Do you believe that? Do you wonder how far God's love will go? Do you wonder if it has a limit? Author Stasi Eldredge addresses this question through the following story in her book *Your Captivating Heart:*

> Sarah was sixteen years old and the adventure of the day beckoned her to come, enjoy, explore! She was supposed to go to school, but Sarah spent the day in the rugged and stunning mountains instead. It had been a glorious day. Driving home in the early evening Sarah's thoughts wandered. She felt so at home in the mountains, so refreshed. Suddenly, a car flashed into Sarah's view as it ran a red light and struck her car head on.
>
> The force of the impact sent Sarah, who was not wearing a seat belt, crashing headfirst through the windshield. As she flew through the air, her left knee caught her, and then thrust her back through the broken glass into the smashed front seat of her car.

Badly hurt and bleeding profusely, Sarah's stunned mind took awhile to kick into gear. Her first thoughts were, I deserved this. If I hadn't skipped school, this never would have happened. Wounded and bleeding, she believed it was her fault . . .

As fate would have it, Sarah's next-door neighbor was in the car behind her and witnessed the whole accident. Using her cell phone, she called Sarah's parents as they were getting ready for dinner. "You'd better come down here. Sarah's been in an accident," she told Sarah's father. The neighbor's calmness led Sarah's dad to imagine a mere fender bender, and so with irritation and no rush, he drove to the intersection to help with the insurance paperwork.

The situation he had anticipated was not the one he arrived to find.

When Sarah's father pulled up to the intersection, he found police cars, fire trucks, and ambulances. He saw the smashed car of the other driver . . . and he saw his daughter's car, utterly demolished. Walking toward it with fear, he could see Sarah in the front seat. Sarah could see him as well and she began to yell out, "Daddy, it's not my fault! Daddy, it's not my fault!"

"I can see that!" he assured. What he could also see were the firefighters trying to use the Jaws of Life to remove the door from the car so they could extricate Sarah from the tangled metal, but the hydraulic tools weren't working. Precious minutes passed. The Jaws of Life were literally not cutting it.

So Sarah's father took action. With fierce passion and love for his daughter, he pushed the firefighters aside, and with his bare hands he ripped the door from the car.

True story.

In that moment, Sarah's father forever answered her question of whether or not she was loved by him. Did he delight in her? Would he protect her, fight for her? Was she worth it? Yes, yes, and forever yes![31]

This is the love that Jesus has for you. He fought the demons of darkness for your sake. There is no limit to his love.

Just as Sarah was trapped in her car, we are trapped in the snare of sin. We can't get out on our own. God knew that even with our best efforts at holiness we still weren't going to be able to pull our way out of the mess that sin has created in our world and in our hearts. Our best efforts would still fall short of the standard of holiness that God had set for those who are going to spend eternity with him.

So what did God do? He decided to send a prince to rescue us. This Prince of Peace came to pull us out of our devastating state of sin, and to restore us to a place of purity, hope, and forgiveness, and a renewed relationship with God.

Rescuing you was worth everything to him. What did it cost Jesus to rescue you? How much does he love you? To answer this question, just look at the cross.

When Jesus was mocked and scorned by the religious leaders, he thought, "You, my beloved daughter, are worth it."

When his flesh was ripped from his back as he was flogged, he knew your rescue was worth that price.

When he carried his cross on his bleeding back, thoughts of you kept him going.

When he hung on the cross, every breath filled with excruciating pain, knowing that he needed only say a word and angels would come and rescue him, thoughts of you kept him there.

He loved you so much that no pain, no scorn, not even death distracted him from the purpose of fighting for you.

You were made to be loved. Loved for who you are, not for what you do. Loved in the core of your being, the good and bad together—unconditional love. You may seek that love in all sorts of places, but the only one who will ever be able to consistently love you that way is Jesus. Can you offer your heart to him?

Each of us was created with a God-shaped vacuum that only God can fill. Saint Augustine said, "You made us for yourself, and our heart is restless until it finds its place of rest in you."[32] But what you may not realize is that God has a place in his heart that you alone can fill. George MacDonald wrote, "It follows that there is also a chamber in God himself, into which none can enter but the one, the individual."[33] You.

You see, God wants the same thing that you want: to be loved. He longs for total intimacy with you. He asks you to let him be the one who guards your heart. Will you let him in? Will you ask him to enter that sacred place within you? If you do, he will come gently. He'll flood you with his love and mercy. I pray you can entrust the one thing he most desires to the one who gave everything to fight for you: your heart. He'll guard, heal, and fill it in a way that will bring transformation and peace.

PRIORITY
3

YOUR MARRIAGE

"Wait a minute," some of you are saying. "Why is marriage the next priority? Shouldn't it be my kids? Aren't they the ones who need me the most?" Someone once told me that when you have a child, from that day forward, your heart is going to be walking around in somebody else's body. I really get that. But what happens when we allow our identity to be rooted in our mothering? What happens when we put our kids before our husbands? It may all work out in the short term, but in the long run, we end up with regrets.

Talking about marriage can hit a raw nerve within us. Oftentimes, this is the area of life where we have experienced the most disappointment and difficulty. It's the area where we most need redemption and hope. So here's the good news: Our God is all about fresh starts. He loves to take us where we are and breathe new life into our circumstances. No matter where we're coming from, God can do something different in our lives from this day forward. I love the verse from Isaiah 42:19: "See, I am doing something new! Now it springs forth, do you not perceive it? In the wilderness I make a way, in the wastelands, rivers." God can write straight with crooked lines. So regardless of what has occurred in the past or is happening in your present, there is always hope. The hardest aspects of our lives, marriage included, can be redeemed.

I remember well a lovely summer day in 1991 in Minneapolis. My boyfriend had flown in from England, and we went to Mass together on the way home from the airport. The sermon was on marriage, which I found interesting, although it seemed to have an odd effect on my boyfriend, Leo. He was fidgeting and constantly looking at me. I later understood why, because after Mass ended, he asked if we could go up to the front and pray. As I was kneeling next to him, he took my hand and said, "If I promise to make you happy for the rest of your life, will you marry me?" How could I say no to an offer like that? If only I'd been able to record what he said. The deal was, if I said yes, he'd make me happy for always! So no one can fault me for entering marriage with that expectation.

We moved to Germany immediately following our honeymoon, and in no time I found out I was pregnant with our first child, Amy. I was sick, and I was lonely. I couldn't speak German, I had no friends, and Leo traveled five days a week. It wasn't long before I sat Leo down and informed him that there was a problem with our "deal." I wasn't happy! I then sat back to see how he would respond. To my great surprise and horror, he became very irritated and asked if I expected him to quit his job and just sit home with me. Regardless of what he had said when he was proposing, he had no intention of taking on the responsibility of my personal happiness. I did not consider this good news.

I had come into my marriage with expectations. I had left behind my family, my friends, my church, and my country when I got married. This left a huge void, and I expected Leo to fill it. I figured he should be grateful that I had been so accommodating.

While the fact that Leo didn't even *try* to fill that void was very upsetting to me, it actually saved the two of us a great deal of heartache, because in attempting to fill that void in my life he most certainly would have failed.

I needed to learn that the void that was in my life was to be filled by a relationship with Jesus Christ. No other man, or person, would be able to satisfy me. The late Ruth Bell Graham states it well:

"It is a foolish woman who expects her husband to be to her that which only Jesus Christ Himself can be: always ready to forgive, totally understanding, unendingly patient, invariably tender and loving, unfailing in every area, anticipating every need, and making more than adequate provision. Such expectations put a man under an impossible strain."[34]

This does not mean that our relationships with other people, especially our husbands, do not affect us deeply. They certainly do. But even the best relationship with a nearly perfect man will never fill the void that is inside us.

THE MOST IMPORTANT RELATIONSHIP

If we want to experience a marriage that is transformed by grace, we need to start with our relationship with Christ. What does it mean to have a relationship with Jesus Christ? It is not the same thing as faithfully attending Mass. It's not the same thing as keeping the Ten Commandments. It's not the same thing as being a good person.

I believe it's helpful to think about a personal relationship with Christ the way we would think of an earthly friendship. Friendships start with getting to know things about one another, and then relationships grow as time is spent together. It's the hours spent sharing from our hearts, and the experiences and memories we make together, that create a special friendship.

As we look at having a personal relationship or an intimate friendship with Christ, we can have feelings of hesitation. He may seem like an unknown entity. We don't know him the way we know our best friends here on earth. But if we take the time to get to know him, and then spend time with him in prayer, he will become the best friend we could ever have. He will never move away. He promises, "I will never leave you or forsake you." He'll never betray you. He'll always love you. He wants what is best for you.

The same can't always be said of husbands, or of wives, for that matter. We all have heard the statistics regarding infidelity and divorce. Christians aren't immune to these heartaches. Many of us have experienced the agony of the betrayal, loneliness, anger, and fear that results from a marital affair or a divorce. Our source of happiness and security must come from something other than our marriages. This is why it's so important that Priority No. 1, God, comes before Priority No. 3, our marriages.

Having a personal relationship with Christ is an incredible gift that God offers us. But we need to take that first step of friendship, and start getting to know him. There's no point in getting to know the Jesus of your imagination, yet that is so often what people do.

One of the important things to learn about Jesus is that he is interested in fixing your relationship with God, the Father. When sin entered the world through Adam and Eve, the beautiful relationship that man had experienced with God was damaged. The perfect unity and friendship that they had experienced was destroyed and a chasm between God and man resulted.

In his commentary on the Gospel of John, Saint Augustine described that chasm like this: Imagine a person on a ship who can see his homeland in the distance. He can see where he wants to go, but there's water in between. This sea is in the way, and there's no way he can get there on his own.[35]

Man might attempt on his own to reach God and spend eternity with him through doing good things, but even the most saintly person will fall short. Because God is perfect, even a sinful thought would prevent a man from reaching God by his own efforts. God knew this, and knew that we would need help if we were ever going to reach him.

Saint Augustine went on to explain that Christ came to the rescue and provided a tree by which a person can cross the sea. This tree is the cross of Christ. No one can cross the sea of life unless carried by the cross. But whoever doesn't let go of Christ's cross will arrive at his *true* homeland, heaven.[36]

Eternal life, union with God, is given as a present. If I give you a present but you take it home, set it on the shelf, and never open it, have you really received the present? No, you haven't. I believe many of us have this present from God sitting on the shelf at home. We were perhaps raised in the Church, went through first Communion, reconciliation, confirmation . . . but have never taken this present from God and opened it up. What does opening up this gift mean? It means that you look at these truths and recognize that they are true for you. You deserve death. You were separated from God. Jesus Christ hung on the cross with *your* sins on him, and paid that price for you. "If we say we have no sin in us, we are deceiving ourselves and refusing to admit the truth." (1 John 1:8) The first step is to recognize that you need Christ. You have to "own your stuff"—admit your sin—and make a break with it. Our starting point must be recognizing our need for Christ.

When you do this, he opens his arms, wanting you to receive him into your heart.

He wants to come into your heart, into the very core of you. This is how he wants you to see the Eucharist. He loves you so much. He longs for complete intimacy with you! He wants to fill you with his Holy Spirit, which will fill you with grace—with strength, love, patience, peace . . . all the things we so desperately desire. When we open the present that God offers us, all of the fruits of the Spirit are inside. God provides what we need to live the kind of life that pleases him.

But we need to move beyond recognizing our sinfulness, asking God for forgiveness, and receiving his grace. God asks us to turn over control of our lives to Christ. He asks us to commit our lives to him, to surrender. We have to make a choice. We have to decide.

Committing my life to Christ means that I am no longer the one in charge. I'll use a car to illustrate the point. I can drive through my life, sitting in the driver's seat, deciding where I want to go and what I want to do. I may even invite Christ to sit next to me. I'll talk to him a bit, maybe ask him to help me along the way, but at the end of the day, I'm calling the shots. That is not surrender. Or, I can get out of the driver's seat, sit in the passenger's seat, and let Christ be the one driving.

For example, say I've just spoken rudely to my husband. Christ, in the passenger's seat, might lean over and say, "Lisa, that was really rude. You need to go and ask Leo's forgiveness and then speak respectfully to him." And I then would lean over to Christ and say, "Thank you very much for your input! I see your point, but you've got to understand, I didn't sleep well last night, and I'm really crabby. This is just how I am today." That's one option. My other choice is to get out of the driver's seat, sit in the passenger's seat, and do what God has asked. Another example involves worry. Imagine that my adult daughter is dating a guy I don't like. I am determined to fix this situation. Christ, in the passenger's seat, leans over and says, "Lisa, you can't fix this one. Your daughter is an adult. You have to trust me. You can't control this one." And I say, "Ohh . . . but I can! You wouldn't believe how well I can control things!" That's one option. My other choice is to get out of the driver's seat, sit in the passenger's seat, and devote my time to prayer and to exercising trust in God.

When Christ is the one in the driver's seat, *he* gets to decide where we go. I don't ask for his advice and help; I *follow* what he tells me to do. *That's surrender.* That's giving over the purple crayon.

This is the single most important decision you will ever make in your life. It's more important than which career you choose or whom you marry. Have you made this decision? Have you turned over control of your life to Jesus Christ? Have you committed your life to him?

Once we do this, we begin that second, wonderful part of friendship, walking through life together, making memories and sharing experiences. Through prayer, we can share our hearts with Christ. He will never get tired of hearing all the little details of your life. This is the first step to having a marriage that is transformed by grace.

Did you enter your marriage with expectations? How have things turned out? My guess is that while some things are the way you hoped, there are areas of your marriage that are disappointments or sources of deep dissatisfaction and pain. So where do you turn with those unmet expectations? You turn to Christ. He sees your needs and desires. Nothing is hidden from his sight. He loves you with an everlasting, unconditional love. He is all-powerful. He is at work in your life, and you can trust him with your hopes, expectations, and needs. He may not always answer you as you desire, but that is why we need faith. We need to believe, without seeing proof of it, that God has our best interests at heart and is at work in our lives. He sees every tear you shed. Nothing in your life goes unnoticed by him.

Mike Mason said it well when he wrote:

> One of the most profound ways in which the Lord touches us and teaches us about Himself and His own essential otherness is through the very limits He has placed upon our relationships with one another. It is an enormous source of human frustration that our need for intimacy far outstrips its capacity to be met in other people. Primarily what keeps us separate is our sin, but there is also another factor, and that is that in each one of us the holiest and neediest and most sensitive place of all has been made and is reserved for God alone, so that only He can enter there. No one else can love us as He does, and no one can be the sort of friend to us that He is.[37]

DON'T SETTLE FOR MEDIOCRITY

No one will be the sort of friend to us that Jesus is. It would be so nice if he were the only influence in our lives—if it were only "the good" that pulled us in one direction or another. But we have an enemy who seeks to destroy us and our marriages. In the event that we think of evil as an abstract concept, the *Catechism of the*

Catholic Church tells us, "Evil is not an abstraction, but refers to a person, Satan, the Evil One, the angel who opposes God. The devil is the one who 'throws himself across' God's plan and his work of salvation accomplished in Christ."[38] No one will be the sort of friend to us that Jesus is, and no one will be as great an enemy to us as the devil is. Jesus wants to transform your marriage. The devil wants to destroy it.

Why is he so determined to destroy your marriage? Why does he care? It's because good marriages drive him absolutely crazy. He knows that God set up marriage as a sacrament. A sacrament is a tangible sign of God's presence, a powerful way in which God pours his divine life into his children. If we live our marriage the way that God desires, then our acts of service and sacrifice will cause more of his grace to be poured into our lives. Marriage is to be a picture to the world of the way Christ loves the Church. The last thing the devil wants is for people to be encouraged by and assured of Christ's love because of a dynamic marriage.

So he sets out to destroy your marriage in many ways. One of those tactics is to tempt you to be apathetic, to be lazy—to look out for yourself, to not give any more to your marriage than is being given by your husband. The enemy of your soul applauds when you think things like, "Why should I give more? I've already given a lot. Why should I forgive my husband? He doesn't deserve it. Why should I encourage him? I can't think of the last time he made me feel good about myself."

The destroyer of marriages will whisper in your ear, "It's good enough! Taking your marriage to that next level, that would take so much work! Let's just leave it as it is." He'll tempt you to settle for ordinary when your marriage could be extraordinary.

93

YOU ARE HIS MIRROR

Get a group of women together and it usually doesn't take very long before someone is complaining about her husband. One person's story tops the next person's, and a good gossip session is on its way. We so often forget that we are the guardians of our husbands' reputations. The way we speak of our husbands is shaping the way those around him see him.

Your husband certainly doesn't want a wife who dishes the dirt on him to anyone who will listen, but he's probably far more concerned about what you think of him than what the people outside your home are thinking. Your husband needs to be believed in. He needs at least one person who will come alongside him in life and build him up. You are that person. Our world is full of people who seem to have it together on the outside but are filled with insecurities on the inside. You may have experienced falling in love with your husband and seeing him as a strong, confident man, only to find that after some time in marriage, the real man emerged, and he wasn't who you thought he was.

He needs you. There is no other person in his life as qualified as you to be his encourager, his cheerleader, his motivator. While women have many of their emotional needs met with other friends, most men do not experience that same level of intimacy in their male friendships. That is often a privilege afforded only to their wives.

How many of us got married, and although we thought our husband was pretty great, we had a little list of "improvements" that we thought our daily presence would produce in him? How many of you have seen those improvements occur? In my experience, no amount of nagging, suggesting books, or making comparisons to men who have it together in that area has done an ounce of good. What I've needed to do is to accept him as he is.

Peter Foster, an air force pilot, knew what a difference a woman's acceptance can make in life. Dr. Paul Brand, who was a surgeon in London during World War II, recorded Peter's story in his book, *In His Image.*

Peter Foster was a Royal Air Force pilot during the Second World War. These men were the cream of the crop in England—the brightest, healthiest, most confident and often the most handsome men in the country. When they walked through the streets of London, people treated them like gods. Girls were jealous of those who were fortunate enough to go out with them.

But the scene in London was far from romantic. The Germans were attacking relentlessly. For fifty-seven consecutive nights, they bombed London.

The Royal Air Force Hurricanes that pilots like Peter Foster flew looked like mosquitoes pestering the huge German bombers. Although they were agile and effective, they had one design flaw. The engine was mounted only a foot in front of the cockpit, and the fuel lines ran along the side of the cockpit to the engine. If the plane received a direct hit, the cockpit would erupt in an inferno of flames. The pilot could eject, but in the one or two seconds it took him to find the lever, heat would melt off every feature of his face.

The RAF heroes who survived these hits would undergo 20–40 plastic surgeries to reconstruct their faces.

The plastic surgeons worked miracles, but still, what remained of the face was essentially a scar.

Peter Foster became one of those downed pilots. After many surgeries, what remained of his face was indescribable. The mirror he looked into daily couldn't hide the facts. As the day grew near when he was to be released from the hospital, Peter became increasingly anxious about how he would be received by his friends and family.

Many of the airmen who had gone through similar injuries had returned home, only to be rejected by their wives and girlfriends. Some of the men were divorced by wives who couldn't accept this new outer image of their husbands. Some men became recluses, refusing to leave their homes.

In contrast, there was another group who returned home to families who accepted and valued them, regardless of their physical appearances. Many became executives and professionals, leaders in their communities.

Peter Foster was in the second group. His girlfriend assured him that nothing had changed except a few millimeters' thickness of skin. She loved him, not his facial membrane, she assured him. The two were married just before Peter left the hospital.

"She became my mirror," Peter says of his wife. "She gave me a new image of myself. Even now, regardless of how I feel, when I look at her she gives me a warm, loving smile that tells me I am ok," he tells confidently.[39]

FOLLOWING JESUS' EXAMPLE IN MARRIAGE

Every day I'm confronted with opportunities to take my marriage to the next level, but I get so tired and busy that it seems like a monumental effort to do anything more than what I'm already doing. I'll be finishing up the dinner dishes and notice that Leo has just sat down in a comfy chair. He *sat down*. And *I'm still up*. I become instantly annoyed. Although Leo has helped get the kids to bed, if I add it all up, I really do have more points this evening. By that, I mean that my day has really been the more demanding one—I'm quite certain that Leo has sat down for longer periods of time than I have, and I do believe his quality of sleep last night was better than mine. My to-do list was longer, and it definitely was easier for him to spend the day with grown-ups than for me to spend the day with small children. Now, I know that Leo would love nothing more right now than a cup of tea, but the last thing I feel like doing is making it for him. I have the opportunity to serve Leo, and to show him I love him, but I'm being tempted to settle for "good enough." Settling for good enough won't necessarily get me into trouble, but it's unlikely to make my marriage extraordinary.

What are your thoughts about serving your husband? Why is it that we will do anything for our children, but we are annoyed at the thought of doing something for our spouses that they are capable of doing for themselves? When we first met our husbands, wasn't it true that we spent time trying to think up ways to delight, help, and build them up? Somewhere down the road, most of us have lost that desire.

Are you concerned that serving your husband is the same as being a doormat? We are not called to serve our husbands because men are superior to women. God asks us to serve them because as Christians, we are asked to serve others. We are called to emulate Jesus and be a servant, as he was. In Matthew 20:26–28, Jesus said, "Whoever wants to become great among you must be your servant, and whoever wants to be first must be your slave— just as the Son of Man did not come to be served, but to serve, and to give his life as a ransom for many." And Saint Paul continued with that teaching in Philippians 2:3 when he wrote, "Do nothing out of selfish ambition or vain conceit, but in humility consider others better than yourselves."

Marriage is one place *among many* where God desires that we set our own wants and needs aside for the benefit of another person.

You may be thinking, "But my husband doesn't deserve to have me serve him." Ephesians 6:7 addresses that concern: "Serve wholeheartedly, as if you were serving the Lord, not men." If you struggle with this, remember that you are living for an audience of one: God. Behave as if his approval is all that matters, because that is the truth.

There is a difference between being a servant and serving. When I serve, I decide at a particular time that I will do a particular thing. I am in control. Tomorrow, I may or may not serve, depending on the circumstances. By contrast, a servant is available whenever the master calls, for whatever the master needs. In Matthew 20:26, Jesus said that if we want to become great we must become servants. And who is our master? Our master is God. This means that we are asked to be available whenever he calls, for whatever he needs. When we pray, we should always ask God to help us to be attentive to the times in our day when he's calling us to set our own needs and desires aside in order to bless our husbands.

THE GIFT OF RESPECT

In his book *Love and Respect*, Dr. Emerson Eggerichs has written about the love women most desire and the respect that men desperately need. He challenges women not to love their husbands unconditionally, but to respect them unconditionally. After speaking on this subject at a conference, Dr. Eggerichs was approached by a woman who asked how she could possibly give her husband unconditional respect. Wasn't respect something earned? What if he didn't deserve respect because of his actions, words, or attitudes? The answer? She was to respect her husband unconditionally in the same way that he was to love her unconditionally. It could only be done with God's help.[40]

Someone once challenged me to see the difference between love and respect by telling my husband that I loved him and then walking away, waiting to see what would happen. I did, and nothing happened at all. I'm sure he appreciated my words, but it didn't seem to particularly set his world on fire. She told me to try again a few days later, but that this time I should say, "I respect you," and then walk out. This elicited a different response. He wanted to know why. Why did I respect him? My words had struck a chord in his heart.

This isn't some new idea. It's as old as Scripture, and was pointed out by Saint Paul in Ephesians 5:33: "Each one of you should love his wife as himself and the wife should respect her husband."

What is the opposite of respect? Undermining, controlling, eye rolling, and manipulating all communicate that we don't respect our husbands. And this can be devastating to a marriage. It can be prominently displayed or subtle disrespect. Regardless, it chips away at our husbands, and erodes their love for us.

99

LET GO OF THE NEED TO BE RIGHT

Every time we are tempted to insist that we are right, we are struggling with pride. I can struggle with this desire to be right in all sorts of ways. I know the right way to load a dishwasher. I know the right way to make a bed. I definitely know the right way to get my kids ready to go out in public. So if Leo attempts one of these activities, I want to instruct; I want to correct. I'm sure this reminds him of someone he knows well—his mother. Now, Leo loves his mother, but he isn't attracted to his mother. I lose sight of the fact that it's more important that I show a heart of gratitude than for the job to be done just the way I like it.

It's hard to let go of being right in the little things. But it doesn't get any easier with the big decisions if we can't let any of these small issues go.

No time in my life was I more tempted to give in to the desire to control and be right than when our son William injured his leg in Mexico at age three. He had been watching his brother's soccer game with Leo, and was playing on a soccer goalpost. He fell, the post came crashing down, and his femur was broken. When I got the news, I rushed to the hospital, just in time to be told that William was going under general anesthesia for surgery. I became completely unhinged, as I didn't trust the medical care there, and hadn't had anything explained to me. Leo tried to calm me down, which made me even more irate. I couldn't figure out any other way to fix the situation, so William did go in for surgery. He came out with a cast from his waist to his ankle.

Unfortunately, something went wrong, and his leg didn't heal properly. William needed another surgery. At this point, my parents did a little research and found the best pediatric orthopedic surgeon in the Washington, D.C., area, and he was willing to treat William. He said time was of the essence, though, and he was concerned that if the Mexican doctor had made a mistake that affected William's growth plate, one leg would be longer than the other. My dad had a friend who flew planes to airlift missionaries out of countries to bring them back to the States for medical care. He was willing to come and get William. I definitely thought this was the best solution. He was willing to come, but we had to decide right away so my dad could arrange things. Leo felt this was a complete overreaction and an unnecessary upheaval. He believed we should trust the Mexican medical system and stay. We have never fought like we did that night. I screamed, I threatened, I pulled out everything in the book, but Leo wouldn't budge. In a fury, I grabbed my cell phone and left the hospital.

I sat outside and called a wonderful friend of mine and told her the whole story. "What do I do?" I asked.

"You know what to do," she said.

"No, I don't," I said, irritated. "That's why I called you."

"You need to go back in there and let him make the decision," she said. "I know that what you are saying makes sense, but you cannot take William out of the country without Leo's consent. Someone has to give. It is doing William more harm to have you screaming over his head than to let Leo make this decision. Let him decide. It will do wonders for your marriage. You have got to trust God in this and let him work."

You see, this was a soul mate friend, and she knew the desires of my heart. She knew that for almost ten years I had been praying that Leo's heart would be set on fire with a love for Christ. I prayed daily that instead of experiencing tension whenever we talked about spiritual things, we would have spiritual unity and strength in our marriage.

It took everything in me, but I went back into the hospital room, and through clenched teeth I said, "You decide."

Leo looked at me and said, "I don't believe you."

I said, "That's the best that I can do at the moment. I'm making a decision to let you decide—to let you lead—and I am asking God to take care of my feelings. I am praying that they follow."

And something in Leo shifted and changed. For the first time in our marriage, he asked me to go and get my Bible, so that we could read something about getting wisdom from God. We prayed together. I was able to hear him asking God, out loud, to help him to make the right decision. Only a woman who has waited ten years for a moment like that can appreciate how precious it was.

Leo decided that we would stay. William had another surgery. I'd like to say that this time it worked. It was actually worse. For weeks William was in traction, literally unable to move an inch. We gave him around-the-clock care, and he slept in our bedroom. In the end, we did airlift him to Washington, D.C. But all of this was done with peace between us. When we finally got to the States, fresh X-rays were taken of William's leg. After studying them, the surgeon said: "You could have saved yourselves a whole lot of cash and hassle if you'd mailed me X-rays before getting on the flight. He's just fine." Incredulous, we showed him the last X-rays taken in Mexico. They clearly showed a leg that was not healing properly. Somehow, while traveling from Mexico to the States, the bones had moved into position and begun to fuse in exactly the place they needed to. I hadn't needed to worry. But God would still have been in control even if William's leg wasn't healed, or never healed. God has the big picture. I do not.

The question is, do you trust God enough to let go? Is your God big enough to see you through? Do you believe that he can take care of you, or your child, in any situation? And do you have enough faith to trust him for your marriage? Are you willing to trust God to make your marriage into a picture of the way Christ loves the Church? Are you willing to give Christ that intimate place in your heart so he can fill it with his grace that will overflow into your marriage? Say yes to Christ, and get ready to watch your marriage transformed by his grace.

PRIORITY

4

REACHING YOUR CHILD'S HEART

When I was preparing to write this book, I had made a list of what I considered to be my most important priorities. I had left it out on the counter, along with other papers. When I came back to grab those notes, I saw that my number one priority had been crossed out, and replacing it was the word "husband" in Leo's handwriting. My son Laeka had come after him, crossed out "husband," and written in its place his own name. They were just having fun (they weren't really saying, "Please don't ever pray again"—they know that would make me the queen of crabbiness), but there was a bit of truth in it. Unless we make a conscious decision to put our husbands before our kids, we will instinctively give our best to our children and give our spouses the leftovers. There's just something about the bond between a mother and child, and the child's need for us, that makes it really, really hard to make our relationship with our husbands the most important one in the family.

Most of us wish that we could give more to our kids. I don't mean material possessions, although that can be a real desire. The gift that we wish we could give more of is most often time. I recently asked a friend of mine what she considered to be the biggest struggle for mothers today. "Guilt," she said. "We all struggle with guilt that we should be doing more."

We read the statistic that working mothers spend an average of thirteen minutes a day in focused attention on their children. Then we read that stay-at-home mothers spend an average of fifteen minutes a day in focused attention on theirs. And we all feel guilty. We feel guilty that we can't provide everything our children want, yet we live in a culture full of entitled kids. Thinking that we are raising entitled kids makes us feel guilty, but then we also feel guilty if we don't give our children the same opportunities that other kids get.

So we get in the rat race and give up family dinners in order to drive our kids to sports and music practices. We run, rush, and generally feel stressed out.

Years ago, I hit the wall as I ran down the path I just described. I had a new baby, but I didn't let that get in the way of getting my other children to their myriad activities. We raced and I did my best to keep it all fair, with each child getting the same amount of activity as the others. One particular day, I dropped Amy off at her piano lesson and ran off to the next child's commitment. When I returned an hour later, I was mortified to see my ten-year-old daughter crying on the front steps of the piano teacher's house. When she got back in the car, she looked at me through her tear-filled eyes and said, "I've been sitting on that step for an hour. When you dropped me off, I went in because the door was open, but the teacher wasn't there. I went back out, and have been sitting waiting for you ever since. I've been so scared."

And I realized we had crossed the line from delightfully busy to crazy. This was out of control. And the only person who could stop the madness was me.

I sat the kids down that night and asked them which activities they really wanted to do, and which they were doing to meet my expectations. I let them each quit a number of things, and announced to the family, "From here on, I am OK with average. Other people may want to pursue excellence through activity, but I'm getting off the gerbil wheel."

If only that could have been a onetime decision, once made and always maintained. But the temptation to jump back into madness comes at me from so many directions that this area of life remains a constant struggle. Can you relate?

Mothers today are overwhelmed with expectations. Guilt abounds. How many of us go to bed at night thinking of all the things we failed to do, or could have done better? For some of us, it carries into the morning, and we dread getting up to yet another day of failing as a mother.

We listen to our culture and take on those expectations. Our children need to get good grades, and we need to facilitate that. Our children must be well rounded—athletic and musical. Yet they need time to play and relax. They need to be well provided for, which drives many parents into debt.

And we want them to be happy. We don't want them to have to experience pain and failure, so we do all we can to cushion the blows and ensure success. My own desire for this became all too clear quite recently. My son was taking his driving test. I wanted him to pass with every motherly fiber in my body. I knew that failing would make him feel rotten, and I so hoped he wouldn't have to go through that experience. The first portion of the test is parallel parking, and if you fail that, you take what is called the "walk of shame." The driving instructor makes you get out of the car and walk around to sit in the passenger's seat, while the instructor takes the wheel and brings the car the short distance back to the entrance of the test area; hence the term "walk of shame."

I had already been through this once with our oldest, and she had wanted me as close as possible, watching her take the test; my presence was apparently an encouragement to her. I offered the same "closeness" to my son, and he told me in no uncertain terms that he wanted me to wait *inside* the department of motor vehicles—definitely not hovering next to the testing area.

So I did what he asked . . . at the beginning. But then I got in trouble for being in a restricted area within the building (I was just trying to look out the window to see how he was doing). So I went outside, but hid behind a tree so he couldn't see me, but I could see him. And it looked to me like he was struggling to parallel park.

My desire for him to succeed shot through the roof. I had already been praying that he wouldn't fail, but it was clear that I needed to call in some reinforcements. So I called my mother. "Mom!" I said. "You've got to stay on the phone with me. Laeka is taking his driver's test as we speak and I need you to pray for him. He's trying to parallel park right now. He's stuck! He can't get it right! Please pray! Right now!" So my mom dutifully began to intercede on Laeka's behalf, right there on the phone. And he successfully parked. My relief was enormous! I told my mom that he was heading out on the road, and I'd call her afterward.

I was absolutely thrilled when Laeka returned and gave me the thumbs-up. He hadn't failed! He'd passed his test! But when he got up close to me he whispered, "What the heck was going on? In the middle of trying to parallel park, all of a sudden I could hear Nonnie's voice coming through the car! I had to beg the instructor to not hold it against me because I couldn't figure out how to turn it off!" Little did I know that even though I was out of sight, crouched behind the tree, I was just close enough for the Bluetooth in the car to intercept my phone call and kindly broadcast it through the speakers. Not my most stellar moment as a mother.

We are also aware that our children aren't really our own—that they belong to God. They are on loan to us from him, and he also has expectations for how they are to be raised. So we do our best to address spiritual issues, but we often feel we haven't done a very good job.

We try to squeeze forty-eight hours of parenting into twenty-four, and we end the day exhausted, focused on what we didn't get done.

But is there any area of life where we are more desperate to succeed? We would give our lives for our children. We do not want to come to the end of our lifetimes having blown it with those we love most.

How do we do what is best for our children, seek their highest good, meet their needs, and truly cherish them? In other words, how do we really love them as God commands? First of all, we have to decide whom we are going to listen to. We cannot be all things to all people. We have to determine whose opinion matters most. Is it what our society tells us? Or is it what God desires?

Recently I was asked where my deep love for God and his words in Scripture comes from. As I thought about it, it occurred to me that the main focus in my home as I grew up had everything to do with this love for God and the Bible. For some parents, the primary goal in parenting is for their children to achieve academic success. For others it is to see their kids settled and happy. Some make sacrifices and ensure that their kids have every opportunity to excel in a certain sport. My parents certainly saw the value in all of those areas of life, but the one area that was a consistent focus was the spiritual growth of my sister and me. In fact, my father wrote each of us a letter when we were in high school, explaining to us what his deepest values were. He went on to tell us what he most wanted to see in our lives. Nothing mattered more to him than seeing his children experiencing a transforming relationship with Christ. In fact, he said that he would rather see us with no faith than for us to settle for a nominal Christianity that showed no evidence of the life-altering effects of the indwelling Holy Spirit. Perhaps the most powerful message was delivered when he wrote that regardless of the success we might achieve as adults, he would consider himself a failure as a father if we didn't have a dynamic relationship with Christ. These are strong words, and they revealed a conviction that informed countless parenting choices as I grew.

If we want to mother in a way that has lasting value, if we want to pass on to our children the things that will really matter in eternity, then we need to determine to reach our children's hearts in the way that God intends and with the truths that God values. It'll mean saying no to some things that are good, in order to say yes to the things that are best.

God gives us this charge through the words found in Deuteronomy 6:4–9: "Hear, O Israel: The Lord our God, the Lord is one. Love the Lord your God with all your heart and with all your soul and with all your strength. These commandments that I give you today are to be upon your hearts. Impress them on your children. Talk about them when you sit at home and when you walk along the road, when you lie down and when you get up. Tie them as symbols on your hands and bind them on your foreheads. Write them on the doorframes of your houses and on your gates."

It's worth noting that these verses do not say, "These commandments that I give to the Church today, or that I give to the school today. . . ." He gives this job to parents. We, as mothers, have the responsibility of teaching our children about God. So often we abdicate this responsibility in hopes that CCD or Sunday school will do the trick. But if we do not take this awesome task and privilege upon ourselves, we will greatly reduce the chance of our children growing up to have living, active faith in God. It is our most important job as mothers.

Look at verse 6: "These commandments that I give you today are to be upon *your* hearts." This is why our first priority must be *our* relationship with God. We can only give our children what we have ourselves. Before we can pass on a spiritual heritage to our children, we need to have God's words in our hearts. Verse 5 tells us which words God wants to be in our hearts: "You shall love the Lord your God with all your heart, with all your soul, and with all your strength." We are to love the Lord, spending time with him, developing and strengthening a relationship with him, and *then* we are to teach these things to our children.

These verses in Deuteronomy go on to show the many opportunities we have to teach our children. We are to teach them when we sit at home, when we walk (or drive) along the road, when we lie down, and when we get up.

God wants us to reach the hearts of our children. Then he wants us to pour his truth into them. How do we do that? We start with effectively disciplining them so their hearts are turned to us and are receptive to what we teach.

TRAINING THE HEART

When we discipline and set boundaries for our children, we communicate love to them. When we don't set limits and follow through with consequences, it causes children to feel adrift.

As much as children appear to be annoyed by boundaries, setting them and insisting that they be honored gives our children a sense of security. Consistent, loving discipline is a genuine display of unconditional parental love.

If we are disciplining our children inconsistently, our authority in their lives will become less and less relevant. Not only will we be dealing with behavior that we don't like; our children will get in the habit of not listening to us regarding how they should act and what they should believe.

Disciplining ineffectively teaches our kids that listening to us is an option. This sets them up for a lifetime of doing things their own way.

So often, we think that the problem is the bad behavior that we are seeing. As a result, we feel like we've done a good enough job as long as our kids don't embarrass us in public. But the real goal of our discipline shouldn't be to just correct the outward behavior. Instead, we want to go deeper. We want to identify what was going on inside our children's hearts when they decided to disobey us.

Luke 6:45 says, "The good man brings good things out of the good stored up in his heart and the evil man brings evil things out of the evil stored up in his heart. For out of the overflow of his heart his mouth speaks."

In *Don't Make Me Count to Three!*, Ginger Plowman describes the heart as the control center of life. She writes, "Behavior is simply what alerts you to your child's need for correction. But don't make the mistake that so many parents make and allow your desire for changed behavior to replace your desire for a changed heart. If you can reach the heart, the behavior will take care of itself."[41]

Teaching your child to change his or her outward behavior without addressing the issues of the heart—the inner motivations—does not get to the core of the problem.

Tedd Tripp echoes these thoughts in his book *Shepherding a Child's Heart*. He writes:

> A change in behavior that does not stem from a change in heart is not commendable; it is condemnable. Is it not the same hypocrisy that Jesus condemned in the Pharisees? In Matthew 15, Jesus denounces the Pharisees who honored Him with their lips while their hearts were far from him. Jesus censures them as people who wash the outside of the cup while the inside is still unclean.[42]

It takes work to help your child to understand what is in her heart, but only then will she will begin to understand her motivations. But how do we do this?

We do this through asking good questions. We ask, "What were you feeling when you did . . . ? Were you afraid of something? Who were you looking out for in the moment? Whose happiness were you concerned with?" You are coaching them toward recognizing the fear, or selfishness, or lack of patience, or desire for popularity or power that led to the decision.

A typical problem with small children is fighting over a toy. The normal parental reaction to a fight like that is to ask, "Who had the toy first?" and then give the toy back to that child. But when you stop and think about it, both kids who were involved in the fight were displaying selfishness. Both had motives for behavior that were fueled by a desire to keep themselves happy, regardless of how the other person felt. In essence, both of the children were saying, "I want what I want, and I don't care how that affects you." A great response to a situation like that would be to shed light on the fact that neither child was treating the other lovingly, and as a result to simply take the toy away.

Once it's clear what motivated the behavior, it's time to talk about what other options were available. God has promised that "[He] is faithful; He will not let you be tempted beyond what you can bear. But when you are tempted, He will provide a way out so that you can stand up under it." It's helpful to brainstorm together about the different ways that your child could have responded. Read this verse together and then ask, "What way out did God provide for you? What other options did you have to deal with this situation?"

After discussing the motive behind the behavior and the other options that your child had, explain the consequence that's going to result. Only give out a consequence that you know you will follow through on. There's nothing less effective than threats that never turn into reality. Threatening to take away privileges and then never doing so simply teaches your kids that you aren't very serious about the rules and standards.

The consequence has to hit them where it hurts. I can remember disciplining Laeka when he was a little boy, and when I told him what the consequence of his behavior would be, he replied, "Fine. I don't really care. Take that away. Whatever." I looked at him and made him a promise. "I will keep going until I find whatever it is that you *do* care about. And don't bother to act as if it doesn't matter. I'm smart. I'll be able to figure out what it is that would cause you the biggest sorrow if it was taken away. And that is what will go. Why? Because I love you that much. I love you too much to let you keep this bad habit which I know will really hurt you in life."

Whenever possible, we should give our kids the chance to walk through and practice the right behavior. Resist the temptation to take things away forever, because they won't be able to exercise the muscle of self-control.

I was recently given the opportunity to put these principles into practice with my older son. My children were getting ready for their catechism class. I had told them what they needed to wear, because not only did they need to look reasonable for their class, but we were going out to dinner afterward. Leo brought them to their class, and when we came to pick them up, I saw my son wasn't wearing what I had asked him to wear. He got in the car, and I began my lecture, which I am sure sounded to him like the adults in the Charlie Brown cartoons. We went home for him to change, and you would have thought I had asked him to peel off his toenails. He made a rude, sarcastic comment as we got back in the car to go to the restaurant.

I was tempted to respond by telling him to quit being so rude and then hurry on to dinner, but I sensed a heart issue going on, so we went back in the house to discuss things. It's always tempting for us to focus on how we feel about what our kids have done or what they have said, or how embarrassed we are. But what we need to do is to try to understand what is going on inside them.

We sat down to address his behavior by talking about what was going on in his heart. I asked him, "What was in your heart that caused you to respond that way to me?" He admitted that he wasn't respecting me, and that he was assuming that regardless of what I thought was the right thing to do, he felt he knew better.

We talked about how there are times that you have to obey, whether or not it seems necessary to you. If our kids can't learn this lesson with us, they are going to have a very difficult time applying that same lesson to God. Think about how often we need to obey God whether or not we understand.

We talked about the fact that God is the one who has decided that I am an authority in his life; I'm not on a power trip. The Bible says, "Children obey your parents in the Lord, for this is right. 'Honor your father and mother.' This is the first commandment with a promise, 'that it may go well with you and that you may enjoy long life on the earth.'" (Ephesians 6:1–3) We expect obedience and respect from our children not for *our* benefit, but for *theirs*. When they obey, it is as if they are under an umbrella of protection. But when they disobey, they move out from under that umbrella and are at risk.

We then talked about how he could have responded. He walked through the right behavior by asking for my forgiveness, and then he got in the car with a better attitude.

You may think, "But it was such a little thing! Was it really necessary to discuss those things over what he was wearing and a rude comment?" I have found that if I take the little things seriously and address them right away, my kids know that I mean business, and it prevents the problems from getting bigger. In the long run it saves time to address these issues when they are small. It also prevents me from disciplining in anger, which is not what God wants.

I'm challenged by Ginger Plowman's words: "We are tools used by God to whittle away the calluses of the heart, keeping the heart tender and inclined to obedience. When we call our children to obey us we are preparing them to obey Jesus, which is our ultimate goal."[44]

What happens when we don't confess our sins? Our hearts grow hard and callused, and we become less sensitive to God and more prone to further sin. In the same way, if we don't address heart issues with our children, and we allow them to get away with their behavior, we are allowing their hearts to grow callous. If we want to teach them spiritual truths, we want their hearts to be as soft and open as possible!

IMPORTANT SPIRITUAL TRUTHS

Before I share the main spiritual truths that I have tried to pass on to my children, I want to answer the question "Why do we need to focus on teaching them these truths, anyway?"

It's a good question.

Kids today face a lot of challenges and problems that can cause them to easily lose hope. The Centers for Disease Control has reported the highest increase of teen suicides in the past fifteen years. A recent survey reported that of the teens interviewed, seventeen percent were at the time seriously considering suicide. The problems they are experiencing seem overwhelming, and they lack the perspective to see beyond them. While on the outside they may seem to have it all together, there is often an inner despair. Instead of feeling an inner peace, many teens feel insecure, lonely, as if there is a hole inside. They lack hope that it can ever get better.

Looking at world problems has caused many teens to lose hope:

- Politically, they recognize that the world has no idea how to establish peace on earth.

- The US economy and national debt make a teen look at the financial future with discouragement.

- They see families falling apart at record rates.

When many of our teens come face-to-face with the inevitability of death, they have no idea where they will go when they die, and don't know how to gain any more understanding about the afterlife, or if there even is life after death. And if this is all there is, what is the point of it all when it involves so much suffering and pain?

Is it any wonder so many teens are lacking hope?

We all want to protect our children from ever coming to a place in life where they have lost hope in the future. But I don't believe that the secret lies in boosting their self-esteem, or making sure that we don't expect too much of them, or making sure that we reduce the suffering in their lives whenever possible.

I believe that the only hope we can offer not just our children but also the world is Jesus Christ. This is how Jesus is described in 1 Timothy 1:1: "Jesus Christ, our hope." The hope that needs to dwell in the heart of each of our children is a person, Jesus Christ.

As we saw in Deuteronomy 6:4–9, the beginning point is ourselves. We need to have not only learned the spiritual truths about Jesus Christ ourselves; we also need to be applying what we've learned to the way we think, speak, and act. Our children are always observing us, and our best teaching tool is our example.

But that doesn't mean that we don't take the time to teach and explain. There are core spiritual truths that we need to teach and explain, over and over again. The following truths are by no means an exhaustive list, but they are the ones that I have focused on as I've endeavored to pass my faith on to my children.

First of all, I want my children to know that there is hope because:

GOD IS THE SAME, YESTERDAY, TODAY, AND FOREVER.

When so much in life is uncertain, when things kids have counted on shift beneath their feet, they can be secure in the knowledge that God is the same yesterday, today, and forever. He will never change. As they get to know who God is, they will meet someone whom they can always count on. I want them to be able to say the same about me, but I'm a limited person, and there will be times that I can't be the mother I want to be. I'll have days when I knock it out of the park, but there will be times when things are out of my control and my kids will need to count on someone other than me. I can't be the foundation they stand on. God can.

So how do we teach our children who God is? All religions look to God, to their creator. What sets us apart as Christians is Christ. We believe Jesus Christ is God. We don't just believe he was a good teacher, or a prophet. As it says in Colossians 1:15–17: "[Jesus] is the image of the invisible God, the firstborn over all creation. For by Him all things were created: things in heaven and on earth, visible and invisible, whether thrones or powers or rulers or authorities; all things were created by Him and for Him. He is before all things, and in Him all things hold together."

And again in Hebrews 1:3: "The Son is the radiance of God's glory and the exact representation of His being, sustaining all things by His powerful word."

Do you want to teach your children what God is like? Help them to get to know Jesus.

When our children are small, we can saturate their hearts with Bible stories. In these years, they are like sponges. Never again will they be so open to learning about their faith. There are fabulous books and media available to help you teach spiritual truths in a way that is appealing to children. Talk about God as you go about your day. When you see something beautiful, pray with

119

your child, thanking God for his creation. When you have needs, big or small, bring them to God in prayer. The more you talk about God, the more natural it will become.

When things don't seem fair, your children can be assured that God sees, and that he is in control. Remind them of this, and read Psalm 11:7 from your Bible: "For the Lord is righteous, he loves justice."

When your children sin, they need to know that there is nothing they can do that would diminish God's love for them, and that he always forgives. Remind them of the truth of Numbers 14:18: "The Lord is slow to anger, abounding in love and forgiving sin and rebellion."

As you teach them about Jesus, remind them that he is who he says he is, and he will never change.

Another truth I've tried to pour into my children is:

GOD WILL ALWAYS KEEP HIS PROMISES.

We need to encourage our children to have faith. God keeps his promises. It's a great teaching tool to share the stories of the Bible that show God's faithfulness. He always does what he says he will do. And the Bible is loaded with promises that he has made to his followers.

He promises to meet all our needs in Philippians 4:19: "And my God will meet all your needs according to his glorious riches in Christ Jesus."

We will not be perfect mothers. We won't always have the right response, or enough time to meet all our children's needs. Instead of allowing this fact to discourage us, let's use it as an opportunity to point out to children their need for God. He is the only one who will perfectly meet their needs.

God doesn't only work through exceptionally talented people. He uses ordinary people who are dedicated to him. Encourage your children by telling them that God will do amazing things in and through them if they will give him their hearts. Ephesians 2:10 reminds us, "For we are [God's] handiwork, created in Christ Jesus for the good works that God has prepared in advance, that we should live in them." This is one of God's promises, and he always keeps his promises.

A third crucial truth I've sought to teach my children is:

THEY ARE UNCONDITIONALLY LOVED BY GOD.

When your child is discouraged, remind him about his true identity as God's child. Your child has a Heavenly Father who is the Creator of everything. He is the king of all the earth. And he's chosen your child to be his prince. Very few people in your child's life will recognize him as such, but in God's eyes, he is royalty.

They don't need to be afraid of God, because of the truth contained in Romans 8:15, 16: "For you did not receive a spirit that makes you a slave again to fear, but you received the Spirit of sonship. And by him we cry, 'Abba, Father.' The Spirit himself testifies with our spirit that we are God's children."

From their earliest days they must be taught that they are God's children, his precious sons and daughters. They must learn that they will only find themselves as they find him. They may try to fill up their hearts with other things, but nothing will satisfy them the way that Christ will.

This final truth is one that I've taught my kids during those times when the task ahead of them has seemed too great. It comes from the children's song "Jesus Loves Me":

THEY ARE WEAK, BUT HE IS STRONG.

I can remember having to talk to one of my sons about the way he was treating his brother. When I laid out the way he needed to change his heart, he said, "I just can't love him like that! I just can't do it!" This was the perfect opportunity to point him to the cross. It was true; he couldn't do it alone. But if he would ask Jesus for help, then God's strength would become his own. We are to use every opportunity to point our children to their need for Jesus Christ. Tedd Tripp says it well in *Shepherding a Child's Heart:*

> The focal point of your discipline and correction must be your children seeing their utter inability to do the things which God requires unless they know the help and strength of God. Your correction must hold the standard of righteousness as high as God holds it. God's standard is correct behavior flowing from a heart that loves God and has God's glory as the sole purpose of life. . . . The alternative is to give them a law they can keep. The alternative is a lesser standard that does not require grace and does not cast them on Christ, but rather on their own resources. . . . Dependence on their own resources moves them away from the cross. It moves them away from any self-assessment that would force them to conclude that they desperately need Jesus' forgiveness and power.[45]

As it says in Philippians 4:13, "I can do all things through Christ who strengthens me." I can't do them alone, but I can do them through Christ. How can we do all of these things? The secret is the Holy Spirit. The Holy Spirit fills us with everything we need—strength, love, patience, peace. Because of this, we can do all things through Christ.

When we try to do things without the help of the Holy Spirit, we usually fail. This is because we are like a glove sitting limp and useless on a table. It isn't until a hand is placed in the glove that any action is seen. The Holy Spirit is like the hand in a glove. We are the glove. He does the work through us.

So, does this mean that if we follow these principles, our kids won't have any problems? Does it guarantee that everything in their lives will go the way they want it to? Look at Paul, the writer of those words in Philippians 4. He was shipwrecked, beaten, flogged, imprisoned, and eventually killed. He suffered. He said:

> To keep me from being conceited because of these sur-
> passingly great revelations, there was given me a thorn
> in my flesh, a messenger of Satan, to torment me. Three
> times I pleaded with the Lord to take it away from me.
> But he said to me, "My grace is sufficient for you, for my
> power is made perfect in weakness." Therefore, I will
> boast all the more gladly about my weaknesses, so that
> Christ's power may rest on me. That is why, for Christ's
> sake, I delight in weaknesses, in insults, in hardships, in
> persecutions, in difficulties. For when I am weak, then I
> am strong. 2 Corinthians 12:7–10

God isn't going to take away all our problems, and he's not going to take away all our children's problems. But each time any of us feel we can't do what he's asking of us, he promises that in our weakness, he will be strong. He will do the work through us.

The way we tap into this power is through prayer. Raising our children to know, love, and serve God is an enormous challenge. Knowing when to say no to good things in order to say yes to the best is hard. Doing all these things when we are tired can feel overwhelming. Prayer is the source of our strength, and the source of our hope. I encourage you to pray daily for your children. It will not only draw you closer to God and closer to your children as you pray for them; it will draw down God's strength and power on your behalf. At the end of this chapter, you will find the prayer list that I have used for years with my own children. I offer it as a resource, a guide, in case you find it helpful.

Four important truths that can give our children hope:

God is the same yesterday, today, and forever.

God keeps his promises.

They are unconditionally loved by God.

They are weak, but he is strong.

As we teach these spiritual truths to our children, we are reminding ourselves of them. When we feel discouraged or even hopeless in our role as mothers, we need to remember that Christ is our hope, and that he has put his Spirit within us. Because of this, we can do all the things that Christ asks of us. Does that mean it will be easy? No. It will demand everything we've got. But aren't our children worth it?

Will you resolve to reach your child's heart in the way that God desires? Will you train the control center—the heart? Will you take the time to teach key spiritual truths?

If you will, then stand back and watch God do his part. In the words of Joshua, "Consecrate yourselves, for tomorrow the Lord will do amazing things among you!" (Joshua 3:5)

MONTHLY PRAYERS FOR MY CHILDREN

I find that it's a constant challenge to balance needs at home and my work with Walking with Purpose. My heart is on fire to enable women to know Christ through Scripture. I want to do all I can to make sure that I have that same focus with my children. I long to see God shape, mold, and fill my children's hearts. These are the prayers that I use daily, month by month, as I lift up my children to their Heavenly Father.

I recommend turning the Bible verses into prayers. Praying God's words back to him is a very effective and powerful form of prayer.

JANUARY

Dear God, my children are being raised in a culture where truth and morals are relative. I pray that my children would know the truth about you, and would follow you wholeheartedly. May they know and love the Bible.

Proverbs 7:1–3: "My son, keep my words and store up my commands within you. Keep my commands and you will live; guard my teachings as the apple of your eye. Bind them on your fingers; write them on the tablet of your heart."

FEBRUARY

Dear God, I pray for holy influences in the lives of my children. Please bring good friends into their lives who will hold them accountable and sharpen them.

Proverbs 12:26: "A righteous man is cautious in friendship, but the way of the wicked leads them astray."

Proverbs 27:17: "As iron sharpens iron, so one man sharpens another."

MARCH

Dear God, I pray for my children's vocations. May they offer you their lives. If it is your will that they marry, I pray they would choose a person of Christian faith and that the strength of their marriage would come from a mutual commitment to God. If it's your will that they'd have a religious vocation, I pray they would say yes, offering you their very best. Either way, I pray they would seek out what your plan is for their lives, and that you'd equip them to fulfill their unique calling.

Ephesians 2:10: "For we are his handiwork, created in Christ Jesus for the good works that God has prepared in advance, that we should live in them."

APRIL

Dear God, please protect my children from evil. I ask for protection from sexual immorality, specifically pornography and promiscuity. Help them to use media wisely, especially Internet social networking sites.

John 17:15: "I do not ask that you take them out of the world but that you keep them from the evil one."

MAY

Dear God, I pray that my children would be leaders in their generation, holding high the causes of Christ instead of the causes of the world.

1 Timothy 4:12: "Don't let anyone look down on you because you are young, but set an example for the believers in speech, in conduct, in love, in faith and in purity."

Philippians 2:12–16: "Do everything without complaining or arguing so that you may become blameless and pure, children of God without fault in a crooked and depraved generation, in which you shine like stars in the universe as you hold out the word of life."

JUNE

Dear God, I pray that my children would respect authority. I pray they'd respect their father and me, teachers, the Church, and other authorities. I pray that their ultimate authority would be you, and that they would surrender their will to you.

Ephesians 6:1: "Children, obey your parents in the Lord, for this is right. 'Honor your father and mother.' This is the first commandment with a promise, 'that it may go well with you and that you may have a long life on earth.'"

Hebrews 13:17–18: "Obey your leaders and submit to their authority. They keep watch over you as men who must give an account. Obey them so that their work will be a joy, not a burden, for that would be of no advantage to you."

JULY

Dear God, I pray that any suffering in the lives of my children would be used to produce holy character. In my role as a mother, I desire to protect. Help me not to get in the way of your work in my children's lives.

Romans 5:3–5: "We also rejoice in our sufferings, because we know that suffering produces perseverance; perseverance, character; and character, hope. And hope does not disappoint us, because God has poured out his love into our hearts by the Holy Spirit, whom he has given us."

AUGUST

Dear God, I pray that my children would be people of integrity (being the same person when no one is looking). Keep them from the faulty belief that you can be one person online and another in reality. Keep them from an obsession with image. May they find their identity in you.

Colossians 3:9–10: "Do not lie to each other, since you have taken off your old self with its practices and have put on the new self, which is being renewed in knowledge in the image of its Creator."

SEPTEMBER

Dear God, as my children prepare for another school year, I pray that they would have strength of character so they can stand firm against peer pressure and the devil's schemes.

Ephesians 6:14–18: "Stand firm then, with the belt of truth buckled around your waist, with the breastplate of righteousness in place, and with your feet fitted with the readiness that comes from the gospel of peace. In addition to all this, take up the shield of faith, with which you can extinguish all the flaming arrows of the evil one. Take the helmet of salvation and the sword of the Spirit, which is the word of God. And pray in the Spirit on all occasions."

OCTOBER

Dear God, I pray that my children would have hearts of compassion. May they desire to serve and meet the needs of the suffering and marginalized. May they be focused on others and free from the mentality that "it's all about me."

Proverbs 14:31: "He who oppresses the poor shows contempt for their Maker, but whoever is kind to the needy honors God."

NOVEMBER

Dear God, grant my children the wisdom to recognize God's truth and Satan's subtle lies. I specifically pray against the following lies:

"What I do on the Internet is my business. It's harmless and doesn't hurt anyone."

"Beautiful girls are worth more."

"I have to perform to be loved."

John 8:32: "You will know the truth, and the truth will set you free."

John 17:17: "Consecrate them in the truth. Your word is truth."

DECEMBER

Dear God, I pray that my children would be careful with their words—not gossiping, exaggerating, lying, or speaking unkindly. I pray that their words would be pleasing to you not just out in public but also in the way they speak to their family members.

Proverbs 4:23–27: "Above all else, guard your heart, for it is the wellspring of life. Put away perversity from your mouth; keep corrupt talk far from your lips. Let your eyes look straight ahead, fix your gaze directly before you. Make level paths for your feet and take only ways that are firm. Do not swerve to the right or the left; keep your foot from evil."

CLARITY IN THE CLUTTER
OF YOUR HOME

The irony of me writing about household organization—gaining clarity in the clutter—would not be lost on my mom, dad, and sister. I grew up in a home with three people who were born organized; I was the fourth. One of my sister's favorite pastimes was to organize drawers for my mom. She used to say to my mom, "Why is it that it takes you and me to get Lisa out the door each morning?" My response was to tell people who came over to our house that when I grew up, I was going to have a messy house full of cats.

But somehow, along the way, I developed a desire to have order in my home. I didn't like losing things, or being embarrassed for people to unexpectedly stop by. I found that I couldn't work well if I was surrounded by clutter, that in order to think clearly, I needed to see order around me. One husband and seven children later, I've developed and borrowed some systems that have been a great help to me. I share them with you here with humility, knowing that there is a great deal that I could learn from you.

Before we dive in, let's put this topic in the context of the other priorities. We all want to be women who have purpose—who know where we are going and what we are doing, and we want to do it with grace and strength. We want our lives to matter. But how often does life get all messed up, and we start to feel that instead of moving forward with strength and purpose, we are putting out little fires and running in circles? So many things call out to us, needing to be tended to, and we don't know what to do first!

Our lives are filled with clutter. We have the obvious clutter of papers, toys, shoes, bags, etc., but we also have clutter in our minds when we have too many things going on and we can't keep it all straight. We have clutter in our hearts when we are resentful, jealous, angry, and unforgiving.

We need to have clarity as to how to sort through the clutter in our lives. We started with God (Priority No. 1), focusing on how essential it is that he has first place in our lives and our hearts. He is the great healer and lover of our souls. When we give God access to our hearts (Priority No. 2), he can start dealing with our soul's clutter, hurt, and need for love.

We focused next on our husbands (Priority No. 3), and the care that we need to give to this important relationship. Remember that we talked about our husbands before we talked about our children. It's always tempting to make our kids our primary focus, but you and your husband were a family *before* they came along, and you will still be a family after they go. Your relationship with your husband needs to be of higher priority than any other relationship in your life, with the exception of your relationship with God.

Our fourth priority is our children. It surprises me how hard it is for me to behave like my children are more important than Priority No. 5, keeping my home organized and running smoothly. This is not because I don't love my children. I really love them and enjoy them, but I have a hard time treating them as I should when I feel like my home is a wreck. It is a daily prayer of mine that I would have order in my home, but that I would keep that priority in its proper place, remembering that things do not last—only people do. And fixing my attitude toward the people in my life is the first step toward finding clarity in the clutter.

THE PREPARATION

MY ATTITUDE

It's so easy for me to fall into the trap of talking to my kids with a sharp, crabby tone. How many times have I heard myself saying, "No, that's OK, *I'll* pick up these dishes that someone couldn't bother to put in the dishwasher. No, really, *I don't mind* picking up your jacket, which you dropped on the floor when you came in the house. You see, *I have nothing better to do* than to pick up after a bunch of slobs. It is my *delight!*" Once I've set that lovely tone in the house, it's only a matter of minutes before the pecking order begins and my older kids start to speak the same way to the younger siblings, and the youngest ones start fussing at each other.

If we want to have order in our homes, we need to let go of keeping track of who is doing the most around the house. Yes, men are just as capable as women of doing housework. Yes, all family members should be contributing. Group participation *is* what we are working toward. But we accomplish nothing when we try to get people to help us by complaining, giving the silent treatment, or doing the work with exaggerated loudness. Your family members will be far more apt to help around the house if you are sweetly helping them. You set the tone for the house, a tone that helps everyone shift from a self-centered focus to one in which everyone is looking out for one another. We need to stop acting like martyrs, and start getting the work done. We need to change our attitudes toward ordering our homes. Instead of viewing it as organizing, cleaning, or planning, I find it helpful to think of it as a way of blessing my family, a way of showing them how much I love them.

Someone gave me advice years ago that I found very helpful. I was newly married, and frustrated that Leo left his dirty clothes on the floor. I felt it was insulting, that he might as well say, "I'm sure you have nothing better to do than to pick up after me." My friend asked me whom the dirty clothes on the floor frustrated. I said that I was the frustrated one. She replied, "Well, if he isn't bothered that they are there, and you are bothered, it seems to me that you would save yourself a whole lot of frustration if you would just take a few seconds and pick them up." I had convinced myself that if I did that, I was somehow degrading myself. But I wasn't. I was just keeping myself sane by attending to the things that bothered me. I was blessing my husband by not making a huge issue out of something that took literally *seconds* to fix.

Many of us entered into marriage considering it a fifty-fifty proposition. But that is not how marriage works. We need to both be giving one hundred percent. Each partner needs to give his or her all to the family. Because I can't control my husband, all that I can do to improve a situation at home is make sure that I am giving my one hundred percent.

As Christians, we are called to be servants. In Galatians 5:13, we read, "You, my brothers, were called to be free. But do not use your freedom to indulge the sinful nature; rather, serve one another in love."

Remember Jesus's words: "Whoever wants to become great among you must be your servant, and whoever wants to be first must be your slave—just as the Son of Man did not come to be served, but to serve, and to give his life as a ransom for many."[46]

Why does God call us to this? Is it because he wants to degrade us? Am I writing these things because I want to take you back sixty years and keep you in the kitchen? Absolutely not. I bring up this issue of servanthood because God thought it was important enough to put it in the Bible, and that's enough to get my attention. If this is the way Jesus lived, why would I think I am so important that I should be treated better than he was?

Yet from a personal perspective, I have found that this is what works. Who wants to have a home that is full of people keeping score of who has done the most? Not I! That doesn't sound like an atmosphere filled with grace and peace.

In John 13, we see Jesus teaching us how to serve one another. It was the night of the Passover, the last supper he was to have with his disciples. They had been out walking, and their feet were dusty. Normally, guests were met at the door by a servant who would wash their feet. In this case, no servant was present. I'm sure that the disciples looked around and wondered who was going to do the job. None of them were going to volunteer—that was the job of a slave! Jesus, without speaking, took off his outer tunic, which left him in the garb of a servant. He then bent down and began washing his disciples' feet. When he finished, he said, "Now that I, your Lord and teacher, have washed your feet, you also should wash one another's feet. I have set you an example that you should do as I have done for you. I tell you the truth, no servant is greater than his master, nor is a messenger greater than the one who sent him." (John 13:14–16) He didn't make a big song and dance of the fact that he was willing to serve; he just did it. And what was the effect it had on the disciples? They were motivated to serve, and later followed Jesus's example, serving him as they shared the Gospel. They turned the world upside down through their service to Christ.

As Christ's followers, we are called to that same level of service.

Pope John Paul II said, "To maintain a joyful family requires much from both the parents and the children. Each member of the family has to become, in a special way, the servant of the others."

We are *all* called to serve one another, but the only person I can change is me. That's where I need to keep my focus. Albert Schweitzer wrote, "I don't know what your destiny will be, but one thing I know: the only ones among you who will ever be happy are those who have sought and found how to serve."

I can have the best organizational system in the world, but if I haven't gotten my attitude in order, my system isn't going to contribute much to the overall peace of my home.

MY PRAYER LIFE

I wish I were the sort of person who learned these lessons and then never had to think about them again. But that's not how I'm wired, and I'd guess it's not how you are wired, either. I need to renew my mind *every day* so that I may start my morning with the right attitude. I know of no other way to do this than through prayer.

One of the primary reasons I try to have an organized home is so I can take the time to start my morning in prayer. If I haven't been organized the night before, I wake up to a mess and start to clean up instead of sitting down and praying. When I do this, my whole day is altered.

What happens when I don't pray?

- I get less done, because I'm not relying on God to help me. God is always willing to step in and help me, but he is a gentleman. He doesn't force his way in. He waits until he is asked. One of my regular prayers is asking God to multiply my time. I have seen him do this more times than I can count. When I rely on him, I look back at my day and can't believe all that I have gotten done.

- I lack focus. I tend to do the things that are screaming for attention first, and I neglect the things that are truly important. Things that I view as interruptions may actually be divine appointments that God has placed in my day. I want to have started my day with prayer so I am sensitive to God's guidance. I need to remind myself every morning that people are more important than tasks, and that at the end of my life, God isn't going to be nearly as concerned with what I have "accomplished" as how I have loved.

- I am less apt to act the way that God wants me to. When I don't start my day with prayer, with a focus on God, then I immediately substitute a focus on myself. I start my day aware of how I want to be treated, of what I want to get done. Instead of seeing frustration and even suffering as an opportunity to rely on God for strength, I react. Someone once told me that the mark of a truly holy woman is that when she is poked the Holy Spirit comes out. What comes out is love and patience. I need to take time each morning to ask the Holy Spirit to fill me up with grace so that I can share it with others.

- I become disconnected from Christ, which means that I am disconnected from my best friend. It's strange—you would think that the longer we are away from Christ, the more we would miss him. But that's not how it works. The longer we stay away from him, the cooler our hearts get. No one loves me the way Christ does, but when I don't spend time with him, I forget that so quickly. If I want to grow closer to Christ, then I need to spend time with him.

When I don't pray, I'm literally starving my soul.

It doesn't take much for our lives to feel like one big mess. But the secret to order is not found in the perfect organization system. Jesus Christ came into the mess of our world for the purpose of reaching into the midst of all of the sin and disorder, to bring each one of us to a place of peace—a place of peace in our hearts and, ultimately, eternal peace.

In our quest for clarity in the clutter, we need to let him into the mess of our lives, and let him create order. This begins in our hearts.

Before you organize anything else in your house, find a place where you can pray each morning. Make sure it's a spot that you like, one that isn't filled with distractions.

THE PROCEDURES

So what are the procedures that can help us to be better organized?

CONQUER THE CLUTTER

The *Oxford English Dictionary* defines clutter as "a crowded and untidy collection of things." Marla Cilley, better known as the Fly

Lady, has written a wonderful book called *Sink Reflections*. In the book, she expands the definition of clutter. She encourages us to consider clutter as "too much in too small a place." This may have happened in your home because your family has grown but your house has not. Or maybe you have simply bought too much stuff. We try to organize clutter by buying big plastic bins, storage boxes, and baskets, but the truth of the matter is, you can't organize clutter. She goes on to write, "Clutter is things that do not bring you joy, you do not love, or you don't need." Too many things that you don't love or need can actually make you feel negative and dragged down. What is her advice for bringing order out of the chaos of clutter? Get it out your door. She insists, "You can't organize clutter; you can only get rid of it."

This is a good thing to remember before Christmas. Because the kids receive gifts from each other, relatives, and us, a lot of stuff comes into the house. It all will need a place to be put away, so I have the children each put twenty things on their beds that they want to give away. This clears space for the Christmas gifts they are about to receive.

When we go through the house bagging our clutter, we try to take it to the car immediately. If it's left in a corner, my kids tend to get back into the bag, and the items get spread all over the house again. Or the bag just sits there and gathers dust.

When my house starts to look as if no one puts anything where it belongs, I call out, "Twenty item pickup!" The kids have learned that this means they each need to pick up twenty items that are not in the correct place and put them where they need to go. I am amazed at how quickly things look better, and the kids don't complain, because there is a clear start and finish to this project. And yes, shoes do count as two items.

I asked my husband what some of our other methods have been to get rid of clutter. He told me that I have no system for our mail. I told him to tell me something *positive*, because no one needs to know about the things that they're *not* doing; they want fresh ideas for what works. So he reminded me that we sometimes get a Dumpster and do turbocharged cleanses of the basement and garage. We're so good that we once threw away an antique bed that we hadn't been using. Mind you, we did it by accident. It was apparently wrapped up in packing paper from a previous move. So I guess sometimes you can get a little over-zealous.

CHILDREN AND CHORES

None of us want to raise children who are spoiled. We all want our families to work as a team, with everyone pitching in. I have tried to keep charts on the fridge with stickers for jobs well done, but found I couldn't keep up with it. I use a different system, which the children can use independent of me, and I can quickly check with a glance. In a binder filled with plastic sheets for business cards, I have a section for each child. Each child has a series of cards that come under the headings Before School, After School, Before Bed, and Weekly Chores. At the beginning of the day, the cards are all facing up. As each task is completed, the child turns the card over. With a quick glance, I can see if the cards are all blank, meaning all the jobs are done, or if some remain. I turn the cards back each night before bed, and leave the binder out for the next day.

Even with this system, bedrooms are sometimes left in a bad state. I can't ignore an unmade bed—it drives me crazy—so I used to go and clean up the bedrooms, getting madder by the minute. I use a different tactic now. I sat the children down and told them that as an extra job, I was offering my services as a maid. If they required maid service, they could hire me, but I was very expensive. I clean up a bedroom for ten dollars. My price goes up if it's a really big mess. This is a lot of money to my kids. On a day when I have had to clean a bedroom, I pick up the kids from school and sweetly say, "Oh, Amy, thanks for hiring me today! You received some excellent maid service from me, and I was really glad to earn the extra ten dollars!" She can either hand me the ten dollars, or it can come out of her bank account. I get the clean room without feeling that I'm enabling laziness in my kids.

THE DINNER DILEMMA

In order to avoid wasting time trying to figure out meals at the last minute and going to the grocery store more often than necessary, I have developed four weeks of menu plans. This process was time consuming for the first month, but the months that followed were a piece of cake. I planned my menu for the first week on the computer. Not only did I write out what we'd have for breakfast, lunch, and dinner; I made a corresponding grocery list. I did this for four weeks, without repeating any of the meals. The month after I did this, I was able to print out my grocery list on Saturday, do the shopping for the week ahead, and never have to worry about whether or not I had the ingredients when I needed to cook. This has saved me a great deal of time.

I also try to prepare my dinner in the morning after the kids go to school. I've found that after school is very busy with activities and kids needing to be listened to, so trying to make dinner at that time is very frustrating.

MANAGE YOUR MONEY

When I was a junior in college, I spent the year studying in England. Things were much more expensive than I had planned, and so I resorted to using my credit card. As a student, I had a credit limit of about four hundred dollars. I remember thinking that I was really able to make a lot of purchases, and seemed miraculously to still be within that four-hundred-dollar limit, because my credit card was never declined. When I returned home, I had letters from my credit card company waiting for me, with the instructions to immediately cut up my credit card and quit using it because I had so grossly exceeded my spending limit.

Heading into my senior year, I knew I had to get a better grip on my finances. I started using a system that I thought I invented, although I have since seen that it is recommended by all sorts of people who are savvy about money management. It's a system that continues to serve me well.

Many people can write a budget, but a budget is worthless unless you can maintain it. I have found that the more I rely on my credit cards, the less I am aware of where I am in terms of my monthly spending. To solve this problem, I used an envelope system. I had a separate envelope for my various expenses. There was an envelope for groceries, one for clothing, children's classes and sports fees, babysitting costs, an emergency envelope for home repairs, one for car repairs, and one called "leisure," which was for miscellaneous expenses. I had a small budget that I had printed from the computer, and I kept it in my wallet. On that budget, I listed the amount of money that needed to remain in my account each month to pay for bills that would come out automatically from my account.

At the beginning of each month, I went to the bank to withdraw the cash I needed to fill my envelopes. Once the money was gone from one envelope, the spending for that category ended. I rarely borrowed from one envelope to make up for a shortfall in another. This gave me an immediate visual cue that I was about to overspend in a certain category.

In recent years, I've used an online version of the envelope system that divides my money into virtual envelopes. Transactions are electronically tracked, and the service links to my bank and credit card accounts, allowing me to keep all of the accounts in order. For those of you who are more adept at using a computer, you may want to try Quicken. This software program allows you to download and track your checking, savings, and credit card accounts.

Your budget and spending categories will be different from mine, but I know that we have the same goal of managing our money in a wise, trustworthy way.

TAKING A BREAK

It might seem strange to consider taking a break an aspect of creating clarity in the clutter. I include it because sometimes it feels like keeping a house in order never ends, and frankly, I find that depressing. If I never get a break, I start to feel like giving up. Once those feelings set in, my systems start to slide.

God didn't create us to be slaves. When he called the Israelite people out of slavery in Egypt, he began the task of teaching them how to be his children instead of the Egyptians' slaves. For hundreds of years, the Israelites had been forced to work without stopping. Their value was based entirely on their productivity. God was now going to teach them that their value wasn't based on what they produced; their value was rooted in their identity. And who were they? They were God's children. One of the ways he taught them how to be free was through the fourth commandment, to keep the Sabbath.

Can you see any parallels today? We live in a world where our value is determined by what we do and what we produce. This means that when we choose to stop and rest, we are doing something countercultural. We are showing that we know we are loved by God, and valued not for what we produce, but rather for who we are. When we say no to activities, we bear witness to the fact that there is someone more important than our schedules—God.

The Sabbath is like a snow day. It's like a day when the shops are closed, school is off, and the roads are too bad to drive on. It's a free day, one with no obligations. You can do what you enjoy! Read a book, take a nap, call an old friend, play a game with your kids. You have permission to play. God gives us fifty-two snow days a year.

On the Sabbath, we are embracing our limits. We're recognizing and affirming that when we stop, the world doesn't end. God is still in control.

I find this incredibly hard to do. I like the feeling of having all loose ends tied up. I feel that if I don't clear my plate, I'll never catch up. I've realized that I'm fooling myself if I think I will ever be capable of being all caught up. There will always be something more that I can do. If I wait until I get my life under control to start celebrating the Sabbath, it will never happen.

When I embrace my limits, acknowledging that I'm going to rest even though I've left things undone, I grow in the area of humility. I'm admitting that I'm not perfect, that I can't do it all, and that I trust God. I'm acknowledging that he is in control of my life, even if I'm not.

When I first decided to try this out, it didn't go according to plan. I woke up on Sunday morning and sat down to pray. Within minutes, I was feeling irritated. There were clothes all over the floor in the laundry room, clutter was everywhere from Saturday fun, meals needed to be made, and the kids didn't have clean clothes that were dressy enough for Mass, or clean clothes for school on Monday.

So instead of praying right away, I thought I'd just get a couple of these things done. Just putting one load into the dryer, just a few dishes into the dishwasher, just a couple of things back in the places they belong . . . and before long, I was mad. I was mad because I'd thought I was going to get some rest, since I'd decided I wouldn't work that Sunday. I figured this whole Sabbath thing was a lame idea.

When I gave it some thought later, I realized that I was missing a very important point that the Jewish people figured out centuries ago. The Jewish people have traditionally celebrated not just the Sabbath but also a day of Sabbath preparation. The day before the Sabbath, they work ahead, to ensure that the following day goes smoothly. I realized that this would be essential for me, as well.

The following week, I announced that Saturday was my day to get ready for the Sabbath. As soon as I got a pocket of time, I did the laundry I needed for Mass and school on Monday. I made sure those clothes were hanging in a separate place, so they'd be ready to go when the time came. I made sure we had belts, dress shoes, and socks, too, since that tends to be what goes missing, causing mass hysteria when we need to get out the door. I decided that it didn't matter if all the other laundry stayed undone for another day; I could do the rest on Monday.

I next focused on food. I figured out what we needed for the meals on Sunday, choosing meals that were simple enough that I could make the food ahead of time. I made the meals and set the table for Sunday morning. I imagined it was Sunday night, and I got everything ready for Monday morning.

I knew that I could ignore undone laundry, but I'm not a person who can ignore clutter. In order to not feel crabby all day Sunday because of the mess, a number of times on Saturday we did "twenty-item pickup."

The next day was truly a day of rest. It surprised me that on Monday morning, even though I had not worked on Sunday, my house was in better shape than usual. But isn't that how it works with God? Through obedience comes blessing. I felt refreshed.

So when we stop for the Sabbath, what do we replace all our normal activities with? We replace them with whatever delights and replenishes us. We can put together a Sabbath box—a collection of toys and activities for the kids that only comes out on the Sabbath.

We also figure out what drains us, and leave those things for another day. What's draining? Being in a rush? Multitasking? Making big decisions? Running errands? Technology? Laundry? Take a break from it. Do something that delights you.

After God created the world, he rested on the seventh day. He delighted in everything that he'd made and said it was "very good." We can imitate God by delighting in what we've been given. Of course, we should do this every day, but it's an important component of taking a break on the Sabbath.

On the Sabbath, we can determine to delight in the little things. As we take a hot shower, we can enjoy how good the clean, warm water feels. We can thank God for the coziness of a fire in the fireplace, or the comfort of a blanket as we nap.

Instead of focusing on their faults, we can delight in our children. Take a look at each of them through God's eyes. He created each of them, choosing what their eyes would look like, what their laugh would sound like, the softness of their skin. . . .

Instead of feeling frustrated that we don't have time alone, we can delight in the fact that our children love us and want to be with us. A day will come when we will long to have their hands in ours.

Delight in the people whom God places in your path. Look at people—really look at them—and try to imagine who they truly are. What might their dreams be? Their hopes? Their hurts?

Of course, the most important component of the Sabbath is turning our focus toward God. Celebrating the Sabbath on Sunday makes sense, as we have the opportunity to go to Mass. In order to most enjoy our time with the Lord, we should keep a spiritual focus on the Sabbath. What are some ways we can do this? It's no coincidence that most parishes offer the sacrament of confession on Saturday. That is an excellent way to prepare for time with God on Sunday. We can make time to pray before Mass, asking God to speak to our hearts in a special way as we receive him in the Eucharist. We might choose to take a walk and thank God for his beautiful creation. We can try to keep an ongoing dialogue with God during the day and make a special effort to pray with our children. We can choose to read Bible stories to the kids at bedtime. We'll be most refreshed if we spend our Sabbath day not just relaxing, but remembering that God is always beside us, enjoying the day and our presence.

If we pursue order and peace in our lives solely through home organizational methods, we will never achieve it. Organization and clutter control should not be our ultimate goals. They should be the means by which we have our homes running smoothly so that we can get on to the real business of living. They should be systems that we implement not so that we can feel proud of how pulled together we are. Instead, these systems should be a routine, a way of life that frees us up to focus on what really matters. And what really matters? How we love! How we love our families, and most important, how we love God.

Let's be like the woman in Proverbs 31, "looking well to the ways of our household." And let's do that by beginning with our hearts. We need an attitude that makes us willing to serve and we need the power of prayer, which will radically transform our days, helping us to create order around us, and most important, within.

FRIENDSHIP

One of my favorite books when I was a child was *Anne of Green Gables*. In the story, Anne is an orphan who comes to live with an elderly brother and sister, Matthew and Marilla. Neither really knows how to deal with precocious Anne and her emotions. Anne explains to them that she is looking for a friend, but not just any friend. She longs for a kindred spirit, a bosom friend. "A what kind of friend?" Marilla asks her, puzzled.

"A bosom friend. An intimate friend—you know," Anne replies, "a really kindred spirit to whom I can confide my inmost soul. I've dreamed of meeting her all my life. I never really supposed I would, but so many of my loveliest dreams have come true all at once that perhaps this one will, too. Do you think it's possible?"

Isn't this the longing of most young girls, and most women, too, if we're honest? We long for a connection with another woman, a best friend who will be loyal to us no matter what. Yet so often what is observed in female friendship is far from an authentic, trusting relationship. All too commonly what we see is women competing, comparing, gossiping, wearing masks, and feeling jealous.

Have you ever been hurt, betrayed, or disappointed by a friend? When we risk it all and share our heart with a friend and the relationship is damaged, we feel the pain deeply.

Nothing kills a good friendship like comparison, because it gets in the way of our being happy for one another, and it plants a seed of bitterness in our hearts that chokes out true love for another person. And how do we make these comparisons? Do I compare my best with your best? No. When I compare, I compare myself at my worst with you at your best. I look at my defects, my failures, my disappointments, and compare them with your pretty haircut, your successes, and your great husband. Do I have a realistic picture of things? No. But that doesn't matter. The harm is done.

When we feel we don't measure up, we often fall into gossip. Maybe we aren't feeling so great about ourselves, but sharing a juicy tidbit about someone gives us a little appeal, makes us a little more interesting. We're feeling bad about ourselves, full of awareness of all the ways we fall short, so we decide to pull someone down with us by shooting a little hole in her reputation.

Often we cloak our gossip in spiritual language. One friend says, "Please pray for Susie. My heart is just breaking for her."

The other responds, "Why? What's going on with Susie?"

"Well, I share this with you carefully, because she shared it with me in confidence. But I'm just telling you so that you will pray for her. Her husband has been cheating on her all over town and she is just a limp rag on the floor! She's just devastated! But don't tell a soul!"

The Hebrew word for *gossip* in the Old Testament means "traveling with a confidence." How that hurts. Proverbs 18:8 tells us, "The words of a gossip are like choice morsels; they go down to a man's inmost parts." Isn't that so true? How often do we forget gossip that we've heard? Not very often. We remember. It was interesting, and whether we wanted them to or not, those words traveled deep within us and lodged in our inmost parts. Just as it's hard to resist a dessert once we've had one taste of the choice morsel, it's hard to shut the door on gossip once we've taken the first bite. We'd be wise to memorize Psalm 141:3: "Set a guard over my mouth, O Lord; keep watch over the door of my lips."

Another problem in relationships with women is our lack of authenticity and tendency to wear masks. And we have lots of them! We have different masks for different relationships, so that hopefully we are liked wherever we go. Many of us have been hurt enough in the past that we are afraid of intimacy. We are afraid of revealing who we truly are. What if this friend proves untrustworthy? Or what if she doesn't like what she sees when she sees the real me? We fear not being accepted. So we put the mask on and go out with our best foot forward. We think, "So what if it isn't the real me? I don't want to be rejected!"

But is a friendship between two women who are wearing masks or comparing particularly satisfying? No. What is the real problem here? We aren't approaching other women with hearts full of love and security. We're approaching them with a desire to have our own needs met. How different it is when we start from a place of being loved—of knowing we are God's beloved daughters, full of grace, a new creation—which can give us the confidence to make ourselves vulnerable. We see that if we are made in the image of God, then we are likable. We have something to offer. We have something to give.

In true friendship we can be authentic. We can be real. A true friendship is a relationship in which we have the freedom to share who we are with someone else and to be truly vulnerable.

In her book *The 10 Habits of Happy Mothers,* pediatrician Meg Meeker stresses the importance of "finding your tribe." "Force yourself to pick a few good women who will go the distance with you," she writes. "Talk with them, write them a note here or there (not an email, but a handwritten note), and tell them what they mean to you. Pick up the phone and chat, even if you can touch base for only five minutes a week. But hang on to those you select for your tribe because you will need them more as you age. And they will need you."[47]

If we want to have this quality of relationship with other women, we need to begin with ourselves. Instead of being frustrated with the way others relate to us, we need to make sure that we are doing all we can to be a good friend. How do we do this? We learn to balance a servant's heart with biblical kindness.

HOW TO BE A FRIEND

DEVELOP A SERVANT'S HEART

From the time we are little girls, we long for friendship. The way we connect, the way we relate to each other is important from pre-school onward. I remember going to my daughter Jane's preschool conference. I asked the teacher how her relationships were with the other girls. She said, "Well, Jane is definitely one of the leaders of the group. Actually, Jane *is* the leader of the group. They pretty much all do what Jane wants. They'll go over to the dress-up area, and Jane will say, 'Mary Grace, you can be the mom; Caroline, you can be the baby; and I'll be the princess.' She's always the princess, but it's OK, because no one seems to mind."

I thought that perhaps there was a lesson for Jane to learn in this, so I talked to her about it at home. I asked her, "If you were to have Annie and Caroline over to play at our house, and there were two shepherd costumes and one princess costume, what do you think you should do?"

She quickly replied, "That's easy. Caroline and Annie can be the shepherds, and I'll be the princess, because I like princess costumes best."

I said, "The thing is, Jane, almost all little girls like the princess costume best. Everyone would prefer that costume. So if you were really wanting to be loving to your friends, what would be the best way to deal with the costumes?"

She thought a minute, then her face lit up. "I know! We'll *share* the costumes. Annie and Caroline could have the princess costume first. It'll be my turn last." ("Great," I thought, "she's getting it!") "That way," Jane continued, "if the moms were late picking them up, I'd get to wear the costume the longest!"

It's hard to put another person's needs above our own. So often we go into friendship with selfish motives. We want to be filled up. We want to be comforted. We want to be encouraged. In Philippians 2:3, Saint Paul challenges us to overcome these urges, and instead "do nothing out of selfish ambition or vain conceit, but in humility consider others better than yourselves. Each of you should look not only to your own interests but also to the interests of others." We are called to have a servant's heart.

What does it mean to display a servant's heart in friendship? We need to be a source of encouragement in our friends' lives. When life gets difficult, we are to come alongside them and build them up. Our words can be powerful tools as we seek to support our friends.

We can see this principle in action in Luke 1:39–55. Mary had heard the news that she was going to have a baby in a miraculous way. When she learned that Elizabeth, her cousin, was also experiencing a miraculous pregnancy, she went to visit her in Judea. How did Elizabeth greet Mary? In Luke 1:42 Elizabeth said, "Blessed are you among women, and blessed is the child you will bear! But why am I so favored that the mother of my Lord should come to me? As soon as the sound of your greeting reached my ears, the baby in my womb leaped for joy. Blessed is she who has believed that what the Lord has said to her will be accomplished!" What encouragement! Think of the whispers of scandal that Mary had been hearing as news of her untimely pregnancy spread. How it must have soothed her heart that Elizabeth didn't just think kind thoughts about Mary—she packed five compliments into her greeting!

And what response did that evoke in Mary? She responded with the Magnificat, a prayer so beautiful and deep that it showed clearly that Mary's focus was on God. And isn't that what Christian friends are to do for one another? We are to help each other take our eyes off of our fears or difficult circumstances and place them on Christ. He is the one who is in control of all things, and he is taking care of all the details.

We also need to be willing to be authentic—to make ourselves vulnerable. Have you ever been in the midst of trouble and thought to yourself, "I can't tell anyone!" That is not healthy. We are to be sisters in Christ, bearing one another's burdens. But we must take off our masks in order to do this. We are called to be authentic, to be real. So you aren't perfect. No one thought you were anyway. The truth of it is, most of us love a person *more* when we see that she struggles just as we do. Then we can relate.

Another way to display a servant's heart in friendship is by rejoicing with those who rejoice, as Romans 12:15 tells us to do. How many friends can truly do this? Sometimes we find it easier to mourn with someone when life is difficult for her. Why is this?

Jealousy is a powerful emotion. Discontent easily invades our hearts. What a gift it is when we can stop competing and comparing, and truly love our friend and want what is best for her! The best antidote for jealousy and discontent is gratitude. What have we received from God that we deserve? Everything good we have is a gift from him. When we compare and feel we have the short end of the stick, and we can't be genuinely happy for the other person, it reveals a heart that feels entitled to more. This is a spiritual problem that is remedied by a focus on our blessings.

If we want to get out of the pit of comparison and self-pity, we need to connect with God through prayer. Every day we paint a mural in our minds. We begin with the background. What is in your background? Is it blue skies and blessings? Philippians 4:8 says it should be. "Finally brothers, whatever is true, whatever is noble, whatever is right, whatever is pure, whatever is lovely, whatever is admirable—if anything is excellent or praiseworthy—think about such things." Is that how you begin your day? Do you start the day seeing God's beauty and love? Do you begin by giving thanks? All the events of the day will be painted on top of that background, but no matter what it is, it'll be wrapped in God's beauty and glory. That's why we go to pray first thing in the morning. Why would we want to spend even five minutes with anything less than this attitude?

When you start with a heart filled with gratitude, you will discover a natural overflow of love from your heart that equips you to be happy for others, even if they have just received exactly what you are longing for. And that is a mark of a true, rare friend.

The second part of Romans 12:15 says, "Mourn with those who mourn." So often, when a friend is suffering we don't know what to say. We seem to typically fall into one of two traps. First, in our desire to be a blessing and to encourage, sometimes we actually wound. Our words can sting an already sensitive heart. I remember losing three babies through miscarriage, and how often kindly intended words brought little comfort. When someone quoted Romans 8:28, "and we know that in all things, God works for the good of those who love him, who have been called according to his purpose," I remember thinking, "I would rather you just give me a hug and say, 'I'm sorry.'" I didn't need a sermon, however short. One of the things that comforted me the most was so simple: A friend gave me a tiny flower arrangement representing something small yet beautiful. She told me that the baby I had held within me was small, but no less valuable than any other life. When a friend is suffering, it can be tempting to point out all the good things in her life to help her gain perspective. Although this comes from a place of good intentions, it can often cause the hurting friend to feel that her pain isn't being recognized.

The second trap we can fall into is to say nothing at all. We're worried that we're going to say something wrong, so we withdraw. But this also wounds deeply, and can be interpreted as judgment or lack of love. We need to say enough to show that we care and we are available, without burdening our friend with advice. A simple "I care. I am here for you. I am praying" means so much.

In the book *The Friendships of Women,* by Dee Brestin, a woman whose husband left her wrote this list of what kinds of things she would have asked for if she could have:

- Contact the person often. Call. If you don't know what to say, ask, "How is your day going?" Write a note. Stop by. (I felt so isolated.)

- Invite her to share a normal activity with you—a walk, a sporting event, an errand, a meal.

- Sit with her at church. She may feel unworthy to join you. Don't let her sit there alone.

- Touch her, hug her. (I am hungry for touch. I miss the physical touch of one who cares.)

- Identify with her feelings. Don't be afraid to mention the other party by name.

- Pray with her and daily pray for her! [48]

In a time of pain, we need our sisters in Christ to remind us of who we are—that we are still women of value, that we are beloved to God, that not only will God not leave us, but they aren't going anywhere either.

BALANCE WITH BIBLICAL KINDNESS

Having a servant's heart in friendship must be balanced by biblical kindness.

In any friendship, there will be things said that occasionally rub the wrong way. When this happens, we are wise to ask ourselves, "Can I overlook this?" Proverbs 19:11 reminds us, "A man's wisdom gives him patience; it is to his glory to overlook an offense."

But sometimes, in order to be truly kind, we need to speak the truth in love. This is different from being negative or critical. If we aren't sure if speaking up about a concern would be biblically kind or if it would be critical and negative, we can look at our motivation.

Why do we feel a need to address this concern? Where are we coming from? Are we angry? If so, we'd be wise to let our anger settle before we speak. Are we confronting our friend because we truly care for her and want what's best for her, or do we just want to get something off our chest? Sometimes this is hard to discern, so be sure to spend time in prayer beforehand. This allows God to prepare your heart by helping you to check your own motivation for the discussion, and gives you the opportunity to ask the Holy Spirit to prepare your friend's heart, as well.

It's also good to remember that we earn the right to be heard. If our relationship has been characterized by criticism, or if distance has meant that we haven't been building up our friend, it's likely that the truth spoken in love will be hard to hear. The majority of our interaction should be binding up, encouraging, and loving. Does your friend know that you would do anything for her, and that you want what is best for her? If not, she is likely to respond defensively to the conversation.

In addition, any conversation like this is best done face-to-face. Letters, e-mails, and texts can all be easily misunderstood.

WHAT TO LOOK FOR IN A FRIEND

We are wise to be discerning in choosing our friends, because as it says in Proverbs 13:20, "He who walks with the wise grows wise, but a companion of fools suffers harm." No matter how strong our personality or how well we know ourselves, we are always influenced by our friends.

Even Jesus gave careful thought to choosing his friends. He spent all night in prayer before selecting his twelve disciples, asking God to help him to discern whom he should surround himself with. He then chose three of the twelve (Peter, James, and John) to be the closest of all. We'd be wise to follow his example. It's hard to maintain a deep level of vulnerability, faithfulness, and support with more than three or four women. When we try to experience this level of friendship with too many women, we often feel that we aren't loving anyone well.

In the words of Meeker, some friends are the "inner-circle" friends, and some are the "outer-circle" friends. [48] Inner-circle friends are the ones who step into your mess without judgment. They fill in the gaps and epitomize the poem by Dinah Maria Craik: "Oh the comfort, the inexpressible comfort, of feeling safe with a person; having neither to weigh thoughts nor measure words, but to pour them all out just as they are, chaff and grain together, knowing that a faithful hand will take and sift them, keep what is worth keeping, and then, with a breath of kindness, blow the rest away."

An outer-circle friend is one who brings you a meal when you have a baby or surgery. She intersects your current season of life, keeping you company on the sidelines of the kids' games or volunteering alongside you when kids leave home and you have more time to yourself. She is important, and your life would be diminished without her. But she is unlikely to know the deeper issues of your heart.

Both types of friendship require tending. Both are incredibly important. But we don't give to or expect from those different types of friendship in the same way.

What is it that attracts you to a woman? Is it her style? Her vibrant personality? Her graciousness? Her kindness? Her obedience to God? Are the qualities you are drawn to superficial ones, or ones that really matter in the long run? When we notice that someone is living the Christian life in a way that we admire, that's a good reason to consider going a little deeper with her; it's an indication that she might be a good inner-circle friend.

It can be a costly mistake to choose someone who has a very different spiritual or moral foundation than you for your closest friend. When the chips are down and you are in crisis, you need a friend who can speak the truth in love and guide you to the right path. Too often, our friends just say what makes us feel good, when they could have been used as instruments in molding us into women of wisdom and maturity. We want to look for a woman who can be vulnerable and real without giving in to negativity. We need to remember that because Christ lives in our hearts, Christian women should approach heartache differently. We should hold on to hope even in the hard times, and this should be seen in the way that we share our hurts and disappointments.

When we find a truly wonderful friend, we need to be sure to keep things healthy. We need balance in friendship. True friendship is different from being codependent or needy. In close friendships, we need to check ourselves to make sure that we don't allow anyone the place in our hearts that has been reserved for God alone. He is the only one who will never let us down. If we place a friend in the position, we are sure to be disappointed. We also need to balance the number of relationships that drain us with relationships that energize us. It's OK to give a lot in certain friendships while not feeling that we get much in return, but if the majority of our friendships are characterized by that quality, we're not going to be able to go the distance.

True friendship and community are hard to come by. Our busy schedules make it especially likely that many of our interactions are superficial. We may have additional difficulty finding a woman who shares our values. The problem isn't always that we choose friends poorly—we might be looking for friends who will help us draw closer to Christ, but we just can't seem to find them. If this is your situation, I encourage you to begin praying about a community of women coming together within your parish for Bible study. I have seen incredible relationships form through these groups. Hearts are transformed through Scripture, masks drop, women support one another in prayer, and friends link arms, stronger because they have one another's encouragement. If this is the desire of your heart, bring it to the Lord. This is a prayer that he loves to answer.

THE DIFFERENCE DIGNITY MAKES

If we don't stop exploiting ourselves and comparing ourselves to and competing with other women, then we are going to be ruled by our insecurities. Our confidence and dignity will yo-yo depending on exterior factors that will always be in flux. Our friendships will suffer as a result.

God is the answer to our quest for dignity, because he is the answer to our need to measure up, and he is the only source for true, lasting security.

It's time for us to stop measuring our dignity and worth by comparing ourselves with other women or whatever ideal we may have in our minds. Our measurements were taken in one place, and one place alone: at the cross. And when Jesus hung on the cross and took your measurements, he decided that you were worth dying for. Was that because of your external beauty, your intelligence, your accomplishments, or your winning personality? No. It was simply because as God's beloved daughter, you were deemed worthy of the greatest sacrifice known to man. What are you worth? You are worth everything to God.

Perhaps you, like me, have had times when you have whispered to yourself, "I'm not good enough. I just don't measure up." Sometimes this follows an experience in which it's clear that someone else sees us as lacking in some way. Please listen to me: Don't give any other person the power to determine the measure of your worth and dignity. There is only one person you should allow to determine that. That person isn't your boyfriend, best friend, or spouse. That person isn't you, either. In all those cases, the measure of your worth can go up and down. The only one who gets to determine your dignity is God. And he already measured your worth.

When you start to feel that you aren't good enough, recognize that you are listening to the enemy of your soul. This is how he is described in John 8:44: "He was a murderer from the beginning, and has nothing to do with the truth, because there is no truth in him. When he lies, he speaks according to his own nature, for he is a liar and the father of lies." There is nothing the father of lies would rather do than discourage us, because he knows it disables us from doing great good. When you think thoughts like, "I don't measure up. I'm not good enough. I'm a loser," stop. Recognize those thoughts for the lies that they are. And replace them with the truth. Say to yourself, "I am a woman of dignity. I am a woman of worth. God says so, and that is all that matters."

When we see ourselves this way, we'll lose the need to compare ourselves with other women, either positively or negatively. We'll begin to look at one another through grace-healed eyes. We'll look at other women and instead of seeing them as our competition, we'll see them as women of dignity, women created by God to be his image bearers. We'll be able to relate to one another without jealousy or masks, and truly love. And we'll discover spiritual sisters who will accompany us on our journey, sharing strength, encouragement, and laughter.

The battle is going to be won or lost in our minds. We are going to need to closely monitor our thoughts, because they will determine our attitudes and actions. How do we experience the renewal of our minds? We need to watch what we're feasting our eyes on. Are we feeding our insecurities or are we edifying our souls?

Filling our heads with images from *InStyle* magazine, beautiful actresses on the screen, and romance novels that make our own lives look pathetic by comparison will not renew our minds. Daily saturation in Scripture will.

Tucked in the thirty-first chapter of Proverbs is the secret to our dignity. This passage describes a woman of wisdom, and gives attention to what she is wearing. I just love the practicality of the Bible. Women pay attention to clothes, and this chapter doesn't disappoint those of us who want to wear the perfect thing for every occasion. While it doesn't disappoint, it might surprise us. This is what the wise woman wears:

Proverbs 31:25: "Strength and dignity are her clothing."

When we think of our insecurities, we probably think about situations in which we fear we'll be vulnerable. We'll be exposed. What an enormous comfort it is to know that because of Christ, we are always clothed. We're clothed with strength and dignity.

When our insecurities start to get the better of us, when something triggers a feeling of insecurity, we can counter that feeling with the truth that we are clothed in strength. This strength is not our own. And thank heavens for that, because when we are feeling exposed and threatened, we're most aware of our weakness and vulnerability. It's at these times that we must remember God's words to us in 2 Corinthians 12:9: "My grace is sufficient for you, for my power is made perfect in weakness." Because of this truth, we can echo Saint Paul's words in 2 Corinthians 12:10: "For when I am weak, then I am strong."

We are clothed in strength and *dignity*. I don't know about you, but when I think of the word dignity, my shoulders go back and I sit up a little straighter. I think of royalty and grace. Our dignity should make us think of royalty, because that is what we are. Because God, our Father, is the king, we, as his daughters, are royal. Our dignity comes from him. It is his gift to us.

The Hebrew word for *dignity* is also translated as *honor*. This is how it's used in Psalms 8:3–8: "When I look at the heavens, the work of your fingers, the moon and the stars which you have established; what is man that you are mindful of him, and the son of man that you care for him? For you have made him little less than God, and have crowned him with glory and honor."

He's talking about us. God has crowned us with glory and dignity. Let's picture this in our minds. Let's picture ourselves with a cloak of strength around our shoulders and a crown of dignity on our heads. If we'll begin each day with this image, if we'll replace the airbrushed cultural ideals with this picture, we will have renewed our minds in such a way that makes us less concerned with our image. As a result, we'll be free to love and our friendships will thrive.

OUTSIDE ACTIVITIES

One of the reasons a book about priorities resonates with each of us is because it sheds light on how we can best use our time. And time feels like it's in short supply! We live in a culture that is obsessed with busyness. I know that each of us wants to use our time in the way that God wants us to. So we've looked at the importance of our relationship with God, tending to our hearts, our marriages, our parenting, taking care of our homes and our friendships.

We've come to the final priority, and we're going to focus on what we should do with all the time we've got left over after we take care of these other things. "What time?!" I can hear you saying. "There isn't any time left!" Well, perhaps *you* aren't saying that, but it's the sort of thing that I think all the time. Then I'm reminded that my life isn't like a neat pie chart. I don't head into each day with tidy divisions and distributions of my hours, giving a certain amount of predetermined time to each area of my life. My life is more organic, constantly shifting and moving. My priorities can't be laid out on a calendar, but I hold them in my heart. They are revealed in terms of what I do first, what I dwell on in my thoughts, and what I am most passionate about.

Many of us work outside the home, and it can seem impossible to give enough time to all the areas of life that have been previously mentioned and not get fired in the process. Please take hope. It isn't impossible. It's most certainly more difficult when you have to balance the expectations and responsibilities that come with a career. But it can be done. The important thing is to choose who will get your best. Our best should always be given to the most significant people in our lives—not our jobs or the places we volunteer. We don't want to succeed in the world's priorities yet fail at home.

Who has our hearts? Whom are we most passionate about? The answer should be our families and friends. But there is an aching world out there, one that is in desperate need of women who see the suffering, pain, and all that's not right in our world. God needs us to see the brokenness and determine to do something about it.

Because there's so much already on our plates, we need to continually choose carefully so we don't take on too much and compromise all that we hold dear. We need to constantly battle the temptation to commit to everything that seems interesting or fun or important. We need to know ourselves well enough to know if we are saying yes to too many things because we are pleasing people and don't want to disappoint. We need to constantly pursue balance.

What qualities are found in a balanced woman? She stands out in the crowd with a quiet confidence. That confidence comes from knowing how very much she is loved by her Heavenly Father, and that he loves her not because of what she produces, but simply because she is his daughter and he is crazy about her. She knows where she is going and stays focused on what is most important, because her prayer life keeps her in constant contact with the Holy Spirit, who gives her all the guidance she needs. She's the best friend you can have, because of her gracious words, loyal heart, and consistent love. Though her circumstances may be difficult, she continues to walk with grace. Where does her strength come from? It comes from within, as God has transformed her heart to more clearly resemble his. This is a woman whom God can use to do great things in our world!

I think a balanced woman is well-developed in four areas of Christian living:

1. spiritual life

2. treating others with grace

3. understanding her faith

4. giving back to help others

Let's look at these four areas one by one. The spiritual life is best described in John 15:5: "I am the vine, you are the branches. Whoever remains in me and I in him will bear much fruit, because without me you can do nothing."

Nurturing and developing our spiritual lives must be our highest priority. And what the spiritual life boils down to is establishing and maintaining an intimate friendship with Jesus Christ. Our prayer lives are an excellent gauge for how that friendship is doing.

Just as our bodies need food, our souls need nourishment, too. God feeds our souls with grace through the Bible, the sacraments, and prayer. This takes time, and it must be given the highest priority in our lives if we want to be balanced women.

The second area is treating others with grace. This is the process of developing the basic character traits that should be seen in any person—not just a Christian. Speaking graciously, following through on your commitments, being a woman of integrity (being the same person when no one is looking), having good manners, and taking care of yourself physically all are part of treating people graciously. We also want to increasingly be women who are optimistic, who have an uplifting perspective on life. My spiritual director wisely told me, "Your face doesn't belong to you." How often do you look at your face, at your expressions? Those around you see it far more often. Having a pleasant look on your face is a gift to others. As Christian women, we should go through life with a fearless positivity that shows the world the difference Christ makes.

Colossians 3:12–15 shows us what we can work toward: "Put on then, as God's chosen ones, holy and beloved, heartfelt compassion, kindness, humility, gentleness, and patience, bearing with one another and forgiving one another . . . and over all these put on love . . . and let the peace of Christ control your hearts."

To check yourself in this area, ask yourself, "Am I a person I would want to be around?"

The third area of Christian living is an understanding of our faith. Having a solid knowledge of our faith has to do with our intellectual development. The more we know about God and about our faith, the more we will love him. The more we know what he expects of us, what the guidelines are that he has laid out for us in the Bible and in the teachings of the Church, the more we're going to make the right choices. Those right choices will correlate directly with our happiness. If we don't take the time to study our faith, we'll be blown around by whatever the current trends are in our culture, which may take us far from where God wants us to be. And being in the center of God's will is the safest and most satisfying place in the world.

Romans 12:2 calls us to give time to growing in knowledge of the faith: "Do not conform yourselves to this age but be transformed by the renewal of your mind, that you may discern what is the will of God, what is good and pleasing and perfect."

We need to pay attention to what we feed our minds. What are we watching on television? What movies do we see? What books and magazines do we read?

To check yourself in this area, ask yourself, "Do I know more about my faith this year than I did last year?"

The fourth area is giving back to help others. If we want to become more and more like Jesus, if he is our role model, then it's essential that we have a heart of service toward others. Mark 10:45 reminds us, "The Son of Man did not come to be served but to serve and to give his life as a ransom for many."

It can be a temptation to take the fruit of our spiritual lives, our nice ways of relating to people, and our intellect and content ourselves with keeping the benefits of these things for ourselves. Yes, our God is a personal God who loves each one of us, knows us intimately, and desires a relationship with us. But his intention is not that we live in isolation. He wants us to take all that he gives us, all that he has developed in us, so we can better minister to a hurting world. He needs us. He needs *you*.

The world is aching for women who are balanced, who recognize the battle that rages around us. The enemy of our souls would like nothing better than to lull us into the impression that life is what we see. In actuality, there is a whole other world—a spiritual world—that cannot be seen with human eyes.

Saint Paul writes of this in Ephesians 6:12: "For our struggle is not with flesh and blood but with the principalities, with the powers, with the world rulers of this present darkness, with the evil spirits in the heavens."

His words speak of a battle. Of a war. And it is raging around us. Evidence of this is seen in the following statistics:

Fifty percent of marriages end in divorce.[50]

"Current trends indicate that by the year 2015 . . . one of every two American babies will be born to a single mother, and illegitimacy will surpass divorce as the main cause of fatherlessness."[51]

Nearly forty percent of all births in the United States were to unmarried women in 2007. In 1980, that rate was only 18.4 percent. [52]

Thirty percent of all women by age eighteen have been sexually abused.[53]

Do you think that the devil is not involved in this? The devil tempts us, not to join him, but simply to do nothing, to watch and complain from the sidelines.

Every second, $3,075.64 is being spent on pornography.

Every second, 28,258 Internet users are viewing pornography.

Every second, 372 Internet users are typing adult search terms into search engines.

Every 39 minutes, a new pornographic video is being created in the United States. [54]

Internet pornography was cited as a significant factor in two out of three divorces. Sex addiction is going through the roof.

Yet we say that Satan doesn't exist. What kind of a culture are we going to leave our children? What are we going to do about it? It breaks God's heart and he says:

"'Whom shall I send? Who will go for us?' And He waits to see if anyone will reply, 'Here I am, send me!'" [55]

Never underestimate the power of one woman's holiness and the difference she can make in this battle. The devil certainly doesn't. How do I know this? I experience it in my own life. Every day I feel tempted to put the things of God aside for the things of the world. Satan shows us things that are good, but not that good. He wants us to attach our hearts to things that are temporal instead of things that are eternal. He wants us to focus on what we want, on what we feel like doing, instead of what we know is right.

If we're going to be women who say, "Here I am, Lord; send me," then it is essential that we take our holiness seriously. We need to make the choice today, and confirm it daily. Please don't make the mistake of thinking that you can flirt with the devil and still fight this heavenly battle and make a difference in our world. This war requires holy women. A battle is being fought for your heart right now, even as you read. Each choice you make gives a victory either to God or to the devil. It's up to you. Life is a battle. You are the hope.

The world needs you to be a woman of balance. It needs you to recognize the raging battle and then to step out into the brokenness, ready to make a difference.

Do you know that when God created you, he also created a specific work that you are expected to do? There are some specific tasks with your name on them that God wants you to accomplish. Ephesians 2:10 says that "we are God's handiwork, created in Christ Jesus to do good works, that God prepared in advance for us to do."

The key is identifying what those good works are. Bill Hybels guides us toward recognizing them in his book *Holy Discontent*. He writes that God has planted seeds in our souls—seeds of discontent. When we see something in the world that we just can't stand, that may be one of the things that God wants us to do something about. Truly, miracles happen when a woman says, "I just can't stand that anymore!" and turns to God for guidance. When you feel anger, righteous indignation, frustration, and compassion welling up in you, turn to God and ask him, "Is this it? Is this one of the things that you created me to do something about?"

There are myriad things that aren't right in the world around us, but if you could help one group of people, who would it be? What issue gets your blood boiling? What brings you to tears or fuels an inner passion for something to change? Don't allow the immensity of the problem to deter you from making a difference. Before you dwell on the obstacles, try to look at the world through the lens of hope. If you could bring change to one specific area of life, which one would it be?

In 1 Corinthians 1:4 we learn that God "encourages us in our every affliction, so that we may be able to encourage those who are in any affliction with the encouragement with which we ourselves are encouraged by God." This means that God will often call us to make a difference in an area of life where we have suffered. It is a hard thing to revisit something that has caused us pain. But God doesn't just want to heal us from our past hurts. He wants to restore to us what we've lost. He wants to bring good from what the devil intended to use for evil. Miscarriage, divorce, grief, abuse, illness, financial loss—these things and many more are faced by countless people every day. Who will minister to them? Those who have been there are going to unquestionably be the most effective at binding up those wounds.

I remember the day that I discovered the seeds of my discontent. I was sitting in church, seeing people leaving early, faces blank, hearts apparently unmoved. I wondered if there were a lot of women coming to church who didn't feel it made any difference. Could they see how it all applied to their lives personally? Each week, they'd faithfully bring their kids to Mass, knowing it was what they were supposed to do, but secretly, did they wonder what was the point of it all? I met woman after woman who had left the Catholic Church saying, "I just wasn't being fed!" I wanted to do something about it. This continues to be what motivates me to organize my time so that I can help make a difference, even in a small way.

I recently heard the story of a local woman named Katie, who experienced her holy discontent in college. One cold night, she'd had enough of thinking about how the homeless of Baltimore were suffering. She decided she was going to do something about it. So she grabbed some old blankets and headed up to the Block, a rough part of Baltimore with strip clubs, sex shops, and other adult entertainment. So many people there were hungry, so the next week she went back, bringing more blankets, and sandwiches as well. When her father, a deacon at my home parish, realized where his young daughter was going, he decided to go with her, afraid that she was a girl alone in a rough area of town. He has missed hardly a week since, and as more and more people have gathered to help, the city of Baltimore has given them a place to work. Today, many parishes work together with what she started, feeding hundreds of people each week. There are people involved who have found that this is their "one thing." They may not be able to go there each week, or organize the whole initiative, but they can make a couple of casseroles that are carried up to Baltimore.

The story is told of a little boy whose heart was moved by hundreds of starfish stranded on the beach. He began to throw them back into the sea, one by one. A man approached him and asked the little boy why he was bothering. There were so many starfish; he'd never be able to save them all. "What difference are you really making?" asked the man.

The little boy thoughtfully picked up another starfish and threw it back in the sea. "I made a difference to that one!" The point isn't how much we are doing: it's whether or not we have decided to step into the battle, to make a difference in whatever way we can.

If you can't think of anything that really rips you up inside, I encourage you to daily pray, "Please break my heart with the things that break your heart, God."

When you come to a place of recognizing what breaks your heart and where you want to be a part of the change, the tasks ahead can seem insurmountable. If God is calling you to do something significant for him, you will feel that you are unable to do it. That's his intention. He wants you to see that when something happens, it was really him at work *through* you. The enemy of your soul wants you to see nothing but the obstacles. The last thing he wants is for you to stand up and fight, to persevere. He knows that "he who is in you is greater than he who is in the world,"[56] and his hope is to get you so discouraged that you give up. Remember, the darkest hour is the hour before dawn. We need to hold on to our holy discontent. To keep going. To fight for what we know is right. To fight for what we know can be. When you feel your hope waning and discouragement is taking over, it's important to remember that it's not all up to you. I encourage you to memorize Matthew 19:26: "With God, all things are possible"; and 1 John 4:4: "The one who is in you is greater than the one who is in the world."

Focusing on these Scriptures changes our perspective. They remind us that regardless of the obstacles we face, God can bring change. When we feel surrounded by evidence that the darkness is winning, we are reminded that Jesus is the light. "The light shines in the darkness, and the darkness has not overcome it." (John 1:5) No matter how bleak things may seem, there is hope. That hope is not found in our tenacity, although we need to persevere. It's not found in programs, although we need to pursue excellence in planning and execution. It's not found in having the biggest pile of financial resources. Our hope is found in God. He can part the Red Sea, perform miracles, and bring change whenever and however he chooses. As a part of his divine plan, he chooses to allow us to cooperate with him in his story. He looks for women who have willing hearts. He looks for women who recognize that in their weakness, Christ's strength makes all the difference. Are you willing to step out and see him display his strength and power through you?

In the words of Hybels, "Friends, in what other life are you going to go all out? We all have one shot and one shot only to leave a lasting legacy . . . a legacy that says, 'I have been trusted to carry God's message of hope to an aching, fractured world in need, and I refuse to rest until my role in that is fulfilled.' When we do this, we show the rest of the world that the present state of affairs does not determine the possibilities life holds. We can finish differently than we started, friends." [57]

We can set the world on fire!

Your True Worth

Priorities can help us to keep first things first. When we live them out, we increase the likelihood that we'll be content with the choices we make. We'll have smoother schedules and happier homes.

But even when we live them out as authentically as we possibly can (which is an enormous challenge), there can still be seasons of life when circumstances turn the best laid plans upside down. There is no perfect formula that guarantees we can always avoid being harried or making mistakes.

It's important to remember that our worth does not depend on living in perfect balance. God's love for us and our value as women does not go up and down depending on how perfectly we execute a plan and keep our priorities in order.

Holiness isn't measured by our perfection. It's measured by how we love. God places great value on generosity, putting others' needs before our own—a mother getting up in the middle of the night with a sick child, a wife who overlooks the raised toilet seat.

He sees the things that no one else sees. He sees the silent sacrifice. The times you bite your tongue instead of lashing out. The times your work and contribution go unnoticed by others. He sees.

But we feel pulled. We feel the constant temptation to measure up to what the world around us tells us is most important. It's hard to restore our focus to what matters most. It's hard to get our minds to think the way God wants us to think. Saint Paul challenges us with the words "Do not conform any longer to the pattern of this world, but be transformed by the renewing of your mind." [58] Which of your thoughts need to be renewed? What are the messages that you find yourself dwelling on, the thoughts that pop into your mind and bring you discouragement? Do any of these sound familiar?

"My body isn't attractive. I need to lose weight. My value depends on how I look."

"I need to do this perfectly. If it doesn't go well, if I fail, I am a failure."

"I'll never change. I can't kick this habit. I'm a loser and I don't have any willpower."

"My circumstances will never change. I wonder if God really loves me? If he did, wouldn't he answer my prayers and change things?"

"My worth depends on my relationships. If my marriage or a friendship or my relationship with my child isn't going well, then I feel bad about who I am."

What is the wedge that Satan is so determined to drive between the way that God sees us and the way we see ourselves? He knows that if he can influence us in a way that causes us to doubt God's truth regarding who we are, he has taken the first step toward disabling us so that we cannot do what God has called us to do.

We are in a battle, ladies. It's not just that we are in the midst of a cultural battle in which much is on the line. There is a battle in each of our homes. Few people see our failures and victories there, but the people who are watching are those we care about the most.

I spoke on the phone the other day to a dear friend who was feeling the heat of battle in her home. She spoke of her frustration in her marriage, and her husband's lack of interest in making things better. She said, "I guess this is what most marriages are like. Mediocre. People grow distant from each other, and things become more and more about the kids. Maybe this is the best it can be, but I think it's awful and I'm so mad that he won't do anything to make it better."

"I think that is what most marriages are like," I said, "and that's why the divorce rate is so high. Someone is going to have to fight for your marriage. If it isn't your husband, then it is going to have to be you. You can't change him; you can't make him work at your marriage. But before God, you have to give your marriage your one hundred percent."

This is hard. This is her battle. But if she listens to Satan's definition of what she is worth in the midst of it all, she isn't going to have much success. She is going to need to fill up each day with love from God. She's going to have to start each day meditating on what God feels toward her, if she is going to be able to give one hundred percent in a marriage in which she feels like her husband just doesn't care.

And she'll have to remember that God sees the sacrifice that is involved in fighting for a marriage. He knows that there is a lot of self-giving.

It's so easy to feel powerless in a marriage like the one I've described, but there is actually so much that a woman can do. We have a profound influence in our homes.

I have a dear friend who has experienced financial strain for a number of years. She had a choice in how she responded to her circumstances. She could have seen herself as a martyr, complaining to her husband and feeling sorry for her children for all the opportunities she couldn't afford to give them. Instead, she chose to be the keeper of the family's spirit and joy. Her attitude had an enormous impact on the entire family. She couldn't afford to pay for summer camp experiences, so she gave her kids cooking lessons at home. Going to the library was a fun outing. Picnics in the yard perked up the day. She thanked her husband for what he was providing for them. She determined to focus on the positive and lived out Philippians 4:8: "Whatever is true, whatever is noble, whatever is right, whatever is pure, whatever is lovely, whatever is admirable—if anything is excellent or praiseworthy, think about such things." Her children are among the most happy and content that I know, and her husband knows his reputation is safe with her.

God greatly values a grateful heart, habits of self-giving, and a willingness to sacrifice. These are the traits that we want to develop in our children. And if we as mothers don't make a concerted effort to replace what they hear all day with this truth, our kids' sense of worth will yo-yo.

Years ago, when my daughter was in elementary school, we spent a whole year dealing with this issue. Amy had been in four schools in four years. This had been hard on her socially. It had been a particularly rough year, complicated by some "mean girl" interaction. As she started at yet another new school, she was hopeful that a friendship was beginning with one of her classmates. I prayed that this classmate would be a good friend and would look out for Amy. One day at school, when Amy was in a bathroom stall, she overheard this girl and another friend saying unkind things about her. They had no idea Amy was listening, but that didn't matter to her. She was devastated by what she had heard.

When she got home and shared what had happened with me, I did my best to push aside my own feelings and point her toward truth. I told her that she needed to decide today whose approval she was going to go after. If she was going to pursue the approval of the girls at school—and then whoever else was popular later in her school years—she would probably still be seeking this peer approval when she was forty. That's how it works. When we seek people's approval and make that our focus, our work never ends. The goalposts always seem to shift. But Amy had a choice. She could decide to pursue God's approval. She could decide to live every day making choices that made *him* happy. I challenged her to decide. Whose approval was she after? My words went over like a ton of bricks, as you might expect. She said something like, "Thanks, Mom," with little enthusiasm. I figured that they had made little impact.

Fast-forward to later that year, at Amy's birthday party. I had planned what I thought was the best birthday party imaginable. I had put together goody bags that were ridiculously expensive, spending far more than I should have. But I so badly wanted it to go well for Amy! All the girls were coming, and I was so pleased, until I found out that one of the "bathroom girls" had invited every girl coming to the party to a sleepover at her house right after my daughter's party. Everyone, that is, except my daughter. I don't know when I've ever been so mad at someone half my size. And I was mad at her mother, too. To add fuel to the fire, as the girls were leaving, I realized that that same girl and her friend had gotten into the goody bags and redistributed the contents, so that they got all the best things, while most of the other girls went home with pretty lame "goodies." I was mad, and I was crushed on Amy's behalf.

We got into the car, and Amy seemed surprisingly fine. "Thanks, Mom!" she said—pretty cheerfully! "That was a great party!"

I turned in my seat. "Are you serious?" I asked. "Don't you feel bad about the sleepover and the way [so-and-so] acted?"

"It's just not that big a deal," she said. "Don't you remember what you told me? I have to decide whose approval I'm after. I decided I wanted God's approval, and I didn't do anything today that would make him disappointed in me. So I'm OK. It's not that big a deal."

And amazingly, she *was* OK. And she had actually listened. I couldn't believe it. She's now in college, and she is still living according to this principle. She's got a lot to teach her mother.

We can make our focus in life pleasing people and seeking their approval. We can choose to equate holiness with perfection and nicely executed plans. We can define our worth by all sorts of shifting standards. Or we can recognize that even our best efforts will always require a savior to fill the gap.

Thankfully, God provided one for us. He didn't wait until we had cleaned up our act. "But God demonstrates his own love for us in this: While we were still sinners, Christ died for us." (Romans 5:8) This unconditional love is what makes all the difference. As we seek to set a pace on our journey toward eternity, consider what you are worth to him: *Everything*.

Endnotes

1. Philippians 3:12–14

2. Isaiah 43:4 NAB

3. Zechariah 2:8 RSV

4. "James Reddick: Sacrifice of a Father," *Best Motivation* (blog), July 15, 2007, http://bestmotivation.blogspot.com/2007/07/james-reddick-sacrifice-of-father.html.

5. Max Lucado, *No Wonder They Call Him the Savior* (Nashville, TN: Thomas Nelson, 2004), 129–31.

6. Father Aloysius Bellacius, *Spiritual Exercises According to the Method of Saint Ignatius of Loyola* (London, Burns and Oates: 1883), 114.

7. Dorothy C. Haskin, *A Practical Guide to Prayer* (Chicago: Moody Press, 1951), 32.

8. Luke 9:51

9. Richard A. Swenson, M.D., *Margin* (Colorado Springs: NavPress 2002), 196.

10. "Stories Behind the Music: Horatio Spafford's 'It Is Well,'" Eras of Elegance, http://www.erasofelegance.com/arts/music/itiswell.html.

11. Philip Zimbardo and John Boyd, *The Time Paradox* (New York: NY: Free Press, 2008), 162.

12. Joe Calhoon, *The 1 Hour Plan for Growth* (Hoboken, NJ: John Wiley & Sons, 2010), 158–9

13. Matthew 6:33

14. Father Jean C. J. d'Elbee, *I Believe in Love* (Manchester, NH: Sophia Institute Press, 2001), 3.

15. Christopher West, *An Introduction to the Theology of the Body* (West Chester, PA: Ascension Press, 2008).

16. Hosea 2:19, 20 RSV

17. Saint Thérèse of Lisieux, *The Story of a Soul* (New York: Doubleday, 2001), 99.

18. Ibid., 99–100

19. D'Elbee, *I Believe in Love*, 26, 27.

20. Ibid., 59.

21. Saint Thérèse's Act of Offering

22. Isaiah 55:8

23. Archbishop Fulton Sheen, *St. Thérèse: A Treasured Love Story* (Irving, TX: Basilica Press, 2007), 115.

24. d'Elbee, *I Believe in Love,* 86, 87.

25. John 9:14

26. Rick Warren, *The Purpose Driven Life* (China: Inspirio, 2003), 82

27. Galatians 2:20

28. Revelation 2:2–4

29. Max Lucado, *You Are Special* (Wheaton, IL: Crossway Books, 1997).

30. Jeremiah 1:5

31. Stasi Eldredge, *Your Captivating Heart* (Nashville, TN: Thomas Nelson, 2007), 69–72.

32. Saint Augustine, *The Confessions of Saint Augustine* (Grand Rapids, MI: Revell, 2005), 16.

33. "The New Name," Christian Classics Ethereal Library, http://www.ccel.org/ccel/ macdonald/unspoken1.vi.html.

34. Debra Evans, *Blessing Your Husband: Understanding and Affirming Your Man* (Carol Stream, IL: Tyndale House Publishing, 2003), 30.

35. "Tractates on the Gospel of John (Augustine): Tractate 2," New Advent, http:// www.newadvent.org/fathers/1701002.htm.

36. Ibid.

37. Cynthia Heald, *Loving Your Husband* (Colorado Springs: NavPress, 1989), 17.

38. *Catechism of the Catholic Church* (Libreria Editrice Vaticana), #2851.

39. Dennis Rainey and Barbara Rainey, *The New Building Your Mate's Self-Esteem* (Nashville, TN: Thomas Nelson, 1995) 3–4.

40. Dr. Emerson Eggerichs, *Love and Respect* (Nashville, TN: Thomas Nelson, 2004), 44.

41. Ginger Plowman, *Don't Make Me Count to Three!* (Wapwallopen, PA: Shepherd Press, 2003), 33.

42. Tedd Tripp, *Shepherding a Child's Heart* (Wapwallopen, PA: Shepherd Press, 1995), 20–21.

43. 1 Corinthians 10:13

44. Plowman, 75.

45. Tripp, 145–6.

46. Matthew 20:26, 27

47. Meg Meeker, M.D., *The 10 Habits of Happy Mothers* (New York: Ballantine Books, 2010), 28.

48. Dee Brestin, *The Friendships of Women* (Colorado Springs: David C. Cook Distribution, 2008), 113, 114.

49. Meeker, 40–1.

50. "Divorce Rate," Divorcerate.org, http://www.divorcerate.org/.

51. Jennifer Marshall, "Sanctioning Illegitimacy: Our National Character Is at Stake," Family Research Council (1997).

52. Stephanie J. Ventura, "Changing Patterns of Nonmarital Childbearing in the United States," National Center for Health Statistics (2009).

53. "Prevention of Child Sexual Abuse," Trust, http://trustdocumentary.org/prevention-of-child-sexual-abuse/.

54. "Pornography Statistics," Family Safe Media, http://www.familysafemedia.com/pornography_statistics.html.

55. Isaiah 6:8

56. 1 John 4:4

57. Bill Hybels, *Holy Discontent* (Grand Rapids, MI: Zondervan, 2007), 136.

58. Romans 12:2

NOTES

Ordinary Lives Extraordinary Mission
John R. Wood

NOTES

NOTES

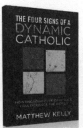

NOTES

Share **Walking with Purpose** with everyone in your parish for as little as $2 a copy.

Order today at **DynamicCatholic.com**.
Shipping and handling included with bulk order.

NOTES

Walking with Purpose®
Enabling Women to know Christ through Scripture

Have you ever thought...

- Where do I find women to connect with who are trying to figure out what it means to be a Catholic women in THIS century?

- I come to Mass and really don't know how it relates to ME?

- My schedule is FULL, I have many obligations, WHERE can I find a place to get some answers?

- Isn't there more to life than just trying to hold it it all together? Why am I HERE?

Walking with Purpose (WWP) reaches out to women who desire to grow in their faith using a Scripture-based program that is fresh, relevant, and focused on conversion of heart more than just intellectual development.

WWP offers leadership training and opportunities for women who want to come alongside others, helping them on their faith journeys.

We begin with the basics, knowing that we can never master the core truths; there is always greater depth to explore.

Find a **Walking with Purpose** program near you or bring the program to your parish!

WalkingWithPurpose.com

Click on "Location" then "How to Start Your Own Parish Program"

Walking with Purpose®

Enabling Women to know Christ through Scripture

Discussion Questions

Visit **WalkingWithPurpose.com** for thought provoking conversation starters for your BOOK CLUB or to challenge yourself!

Also view information on the *Walking with Purpose* Parish Ministry Scripture Studies Program– how to FIND one and how to START one!

You can also find the discussion questions and more *great reading about the Catholic faith* by visiting:

■ DynamicCatholic.com
Be Bold. Be Catholic.®

Find the best in modern Catholic books and learn more about The Dynamic Catholic Parish BOOK Program: an AMAZING way to give a great Catholic book to EVERYONE in your parish.